When Trauma Survivors
Return to Work

When Trauma Survivors Return to Work

Understanding Emotional Recovery

Barbara Barski-Carrow

ROWMAN & LITTLEFIELD
Lanham • Boulder • New York • London

Published by Rowman & Littlefield
A wholly owned subsidary of The Rowman & Littlefield Publishing Group, Inc.
4501 Forbes Boulevard, Suite 200, Lanham, Maryland 20706
www.rowman.com

Unit A, Whitacre Mews, 26-34 Stannary Street, London SE11 4AB

British Library Cataloguing in Publication Information Available

Library of Congress Cataloging-in-Publication Data

Names: Barski-Carrow, Barbara, author.
Title: When trauma survivors return to work : understanding emotional
    recovery / Barbara Barski-Carrow.
Description: Second edition. | Lanham : Rowman & Littlefield, [2018] |
    Revised edition of: When trauma survivors return to work : understanding
    emotional recovery : a handbook for managers and co-workers. University
    Press of America, c2010. | Includes bibliographical references and index.
    Identifiers: LCCN 2017043241 (print) | LCCN 2017050926 (ebook) | ISBN
    9781538105788 (Electronic) | ISBN 9781538105771 (paper : alk. paper)
Subjects: LCSH: Post-traumatic stress disorder—Rehabilitation. | Victims of
    crimes—Mental health. | Helping behavior. | Psychic
    trauma—Rehabilitation. | Life change events. | Stress (Psychology) |
    Adjustment (Psychology) | Personnel management. | Supervision of employees.
Classification: LCC RC552.P67 (ebook) | LCC RC552.P67 B373 2018 (print) | DDC
    616.85/21—dc23
LC record available at https://lccn.loc.gov/2017043241

Printed in the United States of America

I dedicate this book to
the loving memory of my wonderful parents:

Michael P. Barski, 1911–2000
and
Catherine Novelli-Barski, 1911–2012

~

Contents

Part III: Some Special Circumstances

Acknowledgments

In updating and enriching this book, my purpose was to present the most recent research on trauma treatment as well as the thoughts of many experts I have met along the way. This journey has been unforgettable. I appreciate all those who have contributed to this endeavor. I hope readers will benefit from this new information. To many, I owe special debts of gratitude.

First, to my editor, Suzanne Staszak-Silva at Rowman & Littlefield, thank you for your trust in me and your vision. I appreciated your support throughout the re-visioning process.

To my agent, Diane Nine. You welcomed every phone call and answered every email. You were there for me. This project could not have happened—and succeeded—without you. You're the best! I treasure your friendship and guidance.

To Dr. Louis M. Savary, my mentor, guide, inspiration, thinker, and collaborator. I cannot find words to fully acknowledge your contributions to this book.

To Dr. Patricia Berne, an invaluable friend of many years, who provided wisdom, advice, and a guiding presence. This book would not have been possible without you.

To Mary M. McDonnell, an inspiring friend who kept me focused on my vision. Our long evening phone calls discussing my research and progress kept my energy going and helped me to envision the finished product. Thank you for your friendship and belief that I could recreate this book.

To my dance class that includes Tom Pemberton, Ralph Morgan, Dennis Wright, and Eleanor Hodges. You provided an enjoyable, physical movement and companionship to balance solitary periods of intense mental concentration. Also, a special thanks to Don Barrow who encouraged my writing and listened with great interest to the result of my research.

To Maddy Lauria, my researcher and right arm, I thank you for the important role you played with this book.

To Matthew Sagacity Walker of "Everyday Democracy," I thank you for your insight and help in directing me to the new materials available on Dialogue Circles in Pomfret, Connecticut. Our conversations were invaluable. I appreciate your efforts.

To Pat Bragdon, a friend and computer expert who was available when I needed help, I give my special thanks.

To Patti Heynie, my devoted neighbor and friend, whose computer expertise contributed to this book in so many ways.

To my personal and special friends who were there for me: Dr. Michela Coffaro, Evelyn Woolston, Maureen Syntax, Dr. Jeanne Dalton Justice, Donna Ledbetter, and Claudia Catignani.

∿

PART I

UNDERSTANDING THE TRAUMATIC LIFE EXPERIENCE

CHAPTER ONE

~

Why I Wrote This Book

Recent Advances in Understanding Trauma

Since the first edition of my book many advances have been made understanding the treatment of traumatic life experiences (TLE). Society is also more honestly recognizing the prevalence of traumatic illness and its effects among veterans and among trauma survivors at home and within the community.

Statistics tell us that at least 8 percent of Americans (one in twelve) has experienced serious traumatic exposure once or more than once in their lifetime. Fortunately, only about 10–20 percent of these develop the potentially chronic and disabling disease called posttraumatic stress disorder (PTSD).

However, any traumatic life experience can cause upsetting aftereffects that may disturb interpersonal life at home, school, work, and in the community. Research has shown that upsetting symptoms are most evident immediately.

Following traumatic exposure and, for most people, unwelcome symptoms typically dissipate gradually over the following days and weeks.

One of the most helpful advances in the medical and psychiatric fields is the shift from understanding trauma as a form of anxiety disorder. Trauma is now recognized as its own specific category of disease. It is clearly listed as such in the most recent *Diagnostic and Statistical Manual of Medical Disorders* (DSM-5), the standard classification of mental diseases used by health professionals in the United States.

Professional caregivers are beginning to distinguish between a single TLE (such as rape, an armed holdup, or home invasion), and sustained exposure to trauma (such as experienced in military combat or sexual violence in the home). There are also cases where an entire group of people experience a single traumatic event, such as bank employees in an armed robbery or victims of an apartment building fire. Each category requires different treatment approaches.

However, in general, identifying the defining features of this disorder, predicting those who are most vulnerable to it, how to prevent it, and how to successfully treat it remain open questions. Experts from many fields—psychodynamic psychiatry, social psychiatry, biological, cognitive psychology, behavioral psychology, transpersonal psychology, and pharmacology each propose their own models in an attempt to provide approaches to patient treatment.

However, many traumatized people, even those with PTSD, do not seek treatment. Those who do seek it often receive inadequate care or are misdiagnosed and receive ineffective or harmful medication. Nationally, the growth of traumatic experiences in our nation comes at tremendous financial cost and societal loss, since traumatized people, besides receiving inadequate or improper treatment, often develop other diseases, such as anxiety disorders or substance abuse in an attempt to reduce persistent symptoms. These undesirable events include nightmares, flashbacks, hypervigilance, intrusive thoughts, guilt feelings, angry outbursts, irritability, anxiety, depression, limited concentration, and distrust of others. Productive time lost and medical treatments are estimated to be in the billions of dollars annually.

Moreover, despite the widespread awareness of this problem, many survivors still hesitate to talk about their experiences. Women who have been raped are still embarrassed to report it or acknowledge it. Men who have been raped are even more reticent to reveal it. Service men and women traumatized during wartime often refuse therapeutic help unless the mental stress becomes unbearable. Such vets are prone to lose their jobs and their marriages. Many become homeless and a surprising number choose to commit suicide. People traumatized by hearing the diagnosis of a terminal illness seldom wish to have it known by anyone outside the immediate family. People traumatized by job loss or demotion after years working for an organization also feel the same way. I was a manager in a large government agency—a supervisor of eight people and was rifted from a GS-12 position (manager) to a GS-4 (clerk-typist) position. I could not talk about my trauma and sought a therapist to deal with my feelings of loss and grief.

On the other hand, it seems trauma survivors are often wise in their reluctance to talk about their traumatic experiences, because friends and neighbors, coworkers and bosses don't want to hear about it, or even be made to deal with it. In their resistance, some employers, supervisors, bosses, and co-workers would rather deny that any of the people they work for or alongside have such troubles. Instead of helping, they may exacerbate the situation.

Most trauma survivors, unless they require continual or permanent hospitalization, want to resume normal life as best they can. They must learn how to live with their families, how to relate to their neighbors and relatives, and how to adjust to daily job routines in the workplace.

Why I Wrote This Book

This book is not written for therapists or psychiatrists, but for the education of people in the workplace and the community. Its purpose is to offer suggestions on how managers and coworkers can best to relate to employees returning to work after experiencing a TLE. It may also be useful for people in a community with traumatic issues affecting children and their families.

It offers managers, coworkers along with families, and teachers basic human interpersonal skills on how to support the recovery process and how not to interfere with individuals who are returning to work or school or the community after a TLE.

The Challenge Ahead

Few researchers have explored the returning TLE employee experience. And no one, to my knowledge, has studied the powerful role that managers and coworkers can play in supporting the full emotional recovery of a traumatized employee returning to the workplace.

According to Judith Lewis Herman in her book *Trauma and Recovery* (1997) with a new epilogue (2015)—the essence of what a TLE employee feels coming back to work, is *disempowerment and disconnection*. These survivors feel incapable and incompetent to return to their former productive life. They feel disconnected from others such as coworkers, family members, and from the larger community. Thus, such survivors must renew connections with their managers and coworkers as well as with the broader world. This is the only way they can reestablish the interpersonal bonds that were damaged by the traumatic experience.

Dr. Herman offers a process of recovery that unfolds in stages. Naming stages always helps to bring some clarity and order to a process that is painful, complex, and inherently turbulent. While such stages are being "worked through" with a healthcare professional, there are ways that managers and coworkers can support the emotional recovery process.

Understanding the emotional recovery process is central to the structure of this book and forms the basis for the contributions to recovery that managers and coworkers can provide to the returning TLE employee.

While many authors have written books describing the contributions psychiatrists and therapists may make in a trauma survivor's process through the stages of recovery, I have focused on the contributions the survivor's managers and coworkers can make in this process by understanding the emotional recovery process. It helps significantly when fellow employees understand the dynamics of those recovery stages. I have summarized descriptions of this process from trauma into three stages. I have used a simple concept easily understood by the ordinary person to describe each stage.

It is well known that survivors of a TLE want and need at least three things. First, they seek a setting where they can feel safe as a trauma survivor. Second, they need to know that it is acceptable if they want to share their trauma story—or not. Some survivors may want ears willing to listen to their fearful experience. They also want to be sure that no one will pry or probe for details that they are not ready to share. Third, survivors want to feel reconnected to their community—at work, at home, and at play.

The first of the these three stages involves *putting out a welcome mat* for the returning trauma survivor, so such individuals may slowly gain control over their own physical reactions as well as emotional ones. They gradually begin to feel welcome at work and to learn again to manage their environment effectively. A welcome mat is a symbol of a place that is safe and secure. In a workplace such feelings of safety and protection can only be developed through a personal support system. Though the professional therapist certainly provides a context of emotional security and protection for the survivor, the person's family, friends, and coworkers help fill out the team that ultimately must provide this essential atmosphere of safety and welcome.

The second stage is called *lending a listening ear*. Being able to share their experiences helps the survivors integrate both the trauma memory and the circumstances that led to the trauma. As survivors review their story with significant people in their lives, they learn to deal with the traumatic event in a more realistic way. Among a returning survivor's "significant people" are the individual's manager and certain coworkers.

Coming back to work after being out of the office for some time creates uncertainty and ambivalence for some traumatized people, because they really do not know what to expect when they open the office door on the first day back. Still under the influence of their traumatic experience, they may feel unsure how to behave or what to say to other people. Individuals may want to talk about their trauma to colleagues at work, or they may not. However, welcoming them back, acknowledging their situation, and providing a listening ear would be helpful and supportive.

Dr. Bessel van der Kolk in his book *The Body Keeps the Score: Brain, Mind, and Body in the Healing of Trauma* (2014) highlights the power of telling the story:

> Trauma stories lessen the isolation of trauma, and they provide an *explanation* for why people suffer the way they do. They allow doctors to make diagnoses, so that they can address problems like insomnia, rage, nightmares, or numbing. Stories can also provide people with a target to blame. Blaming is a universal human trait that helps people feel good while feeling bad, or, as my old teacher Elvin Semrad used to say: "Hate makes the world go round." But stories also obscure a more important issue, namely, that trauma radically changes people: that in fact they no longer are "themselves."[1]

The third stage in recovery is called *offering a helping hand*. Its primary purpose is to initiate and reestablish the personal connections between the survivor and his or her community. During this stage, the trauma survivor must deal with creating a future, developing a new sense of self and restoring relationships. Emerging from the traumatic environment of uncertainty, survivors may not know how to reach out to managers and coworkers to reclaim their place in the workplace setting. It is up to the managers and coworkers to offer a helping hand, to respond positively and proactively to help restore these relationships. My purpose in writing this book is to show them how to support these stages of healing appropriately.

This third, offer a helping-hand stage, involves relinking the person to the work community. It is very important since survivors of trauma will usually be distracted for the first few days or weeks back on the job. The boss will need to know, for example, when to engage the trauma survivors in reaching certain deadlines and how to gradually increase the workload. It's not unusual that trauma survivors may tire easily, feel confused, or want to escape for a while. For example, a person may want to go for a walk each day or want to participate in an exercise program. Certainly, they may want to check in with their family during work hours. It's important that whatever it is that they want to do, if it is within reason, management will give all the helping-hand support needed during this transitioning back and reconnecting to work activity.

Returning TLE employees exist in all organizations. However, most organizations do not have a method for supporting the three stages of emotional recovery that confront a returning traumatized survivor.

It was apparent to me that what was lacking here was a short-term, essentially cost-free, educational experience that could be conducted on-site, especially for managers who supervise the reentry of such employees. Similar education was needed also for the coworkers of these individuals since coworkers are normally the ones who spend the most time with the survivors. Currently, in most organizations, professional counseling and therapy are usually made available to returning TLE employees. However, there seems to be no complementary, nontherapeutic intervention designed to teach managers and employees about the three stages of emotional recovery from trauma, nor a program that would show them how to create an appropriate ambiance in the workplace for reentry of traumatized employees.

The Dialogue Circle is an adult learning format that can do this. It's different from a focus group or a brainstorming session. A Dialogue Circle provides a learning-plus-action structure so that managers and coworkers can explore a very sensitive personal and organizational challenge in an atmosphere of mutual respect and dialogue. Few other educational processes currently available in the business world can make this claim. The Dialogue Circle can bring managers and employees together, as equals, to examine and discuss these emotional issues and find ways to apply in the workplace what they learn in the Dialogue Circle.

When survivors return to a workplace that provides a *welcome mat* for them, a willing *listening ear* to hear their trauma experience, and a *helping hand* to reestablish connections to the workplace family, they are more likely to recover more quickly and become once again fully productive members of the workplace team.

The rest of Part I of this book focuses on understanding the TLE itself. Part II describes the Dialogue Circle educational process, specifically the sessions on the three stages in the emotional recovery from trauma, designed for managers and coworkers. Part III focuses on some special circumstances, for example, when trauma affects employee's children, when a traumatic event such as a bank robbery simultaneously affects a number of employees, and how traumatized persons can use personal and community resources to help themselves.

Note

1. Van der Kolk Bessel, *The Body Keep the Score: Brain, Mind and Body in the Healing of Trauma* (New York: Viking Press, 2014), 237.

~

CHAPTER TWO

What Is a Traumatic Life Experience?

Examples of Traumatic Life Experiences

Technically, a traumatic life experience (TLE) is a *single unexpected, emotionally and physically overwhelming and utterly unwelcome event.* There are many TLEs. Some may be public and newsworthy, such as rapes, murders, suicides, burning buildings, natural disasters, kidnappings, explosions, terrorist attacks, and hostage situations.

But other TLEs, the ones that don't make the headlines, can be just as devastating personally. Some of these include being diagnosed with a terminal illness, a job or career loss, losing a baby, or having your teenager arrested for drunk driving. Although traumas like this are commonplace and happen to people every day, it doesn't mean they are any less emotionally crippling. We hear TLEs described frequently in more ordinary language. For example:

"When my wife told me she wanted a divorce, it knocked the wind out of my sails."

"When I got fired from my job, it dealt a major blow to my self-esteem and my career."

"When my home was burglarized, it completely wiped out my sense of security. No place felt safe for me anymore."

"When my child was diagnosed with leukemia, it felt like getting punched in the face by a heavyweight boxing champion."

"When the policeman told me my son had been killed in an auto accident, my world came crashing down."

"When I had my heart attack, my entire future felt threatened."

"When my husband died so suddenly, it seemed like the end of everything."

"It may not seem important or tragic to you, but I have lived alone without family for most of my life, and when my Irish Setter Ruffy died, I lost my closest friend and companion for seventeen years."

"When our daughter told us she was pregnant, we were devastated because she was ready to go to college and we didn't expect this news."

"I came into my neighborhood convenience store early one morning and found the owner, old Mr. Saul, dead on the floor. I find I can't go in that store any more. All I see is him dead on the floor."

"After I was raped, I felt utterly dirty and shameful, afraid to look anybody in the face."

"When the court awarded custody of my children to my spouse, I felt utterly powerless and helpless."

"When I was betrayed by my closest friend, my spirit was crushed. He literally took all the money I had and ran away."

"When the doctor told me my baby was diagnosed with Down syndrome, my life was turned upside down."

"When my husband ran off with another woman, I was shocked and enraged. How could I have been so naive?"

"When I was told that I had to put my mother in a nursing home after having taken care of her at home, I felt I was abandoning her."

The list of TLEs goes on and on.

Where and When a TLE Can Happen

Some TLEs happen directly to you, like a sudden life-changing illness, a holdup, or a betrayal of trust. Some happen to those dear to you, your spouse, your children, your parents, your closest friends. Even though many traumatic experiences happen outside the workplace, they still have their effect on the workplace. Their effects are measured in days lost, substandard quality of work, and the inability to perform with accustomed efficiency and effectiveness.

Some traumatic events happen at work, of course. The most newsworthy ones include armed attack by a deranged gunman or an explosion perpetrated by a terrorist. Other group-experienced traumas include break-ins and robberies, accidental fires that destroy the workplace and create panic among those locked inside, or large scale layoffs through mergers buyouts and bankruptcies that leave people without jobs.

The recovery process is often prolonged when many individuals in a workplace community have been traumatized by the same event, for example, the Challenger disaster, the bombing of the federal building in Oklahoma City, or the terrorist attack on the World Trade Center. Although mutual care and compassion can certainly help the healing process, usually some group therapy or group ritual is required to turn the tide toward recovery when a group of employees have been traumatized by the same event.

Recovery from traumatic events experienced by a whole group of employees is discussed in chapter 13 "When a Group Is Traumatized, How Do Managers and Employees Cope?"

What Is Not a TLE

There are many kinds of *chronic* traumas that fall also outside the scope of this book because they are far beyond the abilities of any manager or supervisor to deal with. They require serious and often prolonged medical and psychological help.

Those traumatized by chronic situations include, for example, servicemen and women traumatized daily by facing the violence and bloodshed of military combat and warfare. Children and spouses who have been sexually and physically abused over a period of years are wrenched with fear and anxiety. People who have undergone severe physical and emotional deprivation in detention camps or hard-labor prisons, or even in prolonged homelessness living on the streets, also often have severe emotional issues. People with acute mental and physical handicaps such as personality disorders or quadriplegia that can never be overcome. All of these are traumatic situations, but they are *not* what I am calling a TLE.

In more ordinary, chronically stressful circumstances, certain people today are forced to live and work in continually trauma-producing situations: hospital nurses who work in intensive care units where more patients die than survive; wheelchair-bound individuals continually challenged and frustrated by their handicaps; parents living with a drug- or alcohol-addicted family member; a spouse living with a partner subject to bouts of depression, epilepsy, or schizophrenia; mothers caring for a colicky baby for several months; a single adult child having to care for a dying parent at home, especially one who is critical and complaining; family members living together in quarters that are too crowded; individuals living with a chronic debilitating illness such as asthma, lung cancer, or immune deficiency; diabetics living within a severely restricted diet. All of these are also major long-lasting traumatic situations, but they are not what I am calling a TLE, namely, a single TLE.

In contrast to a one-time traumatic event, the effects of chronically trauma-generating situations limit employees' ability to perform naturally and normally on a continual basis. Usually, none of these employees afflicted by chronic traumatic situations can be helped by the approach suggested in this book. People with these challenges are under such permanent or unremitting stress that the process of "recovery" that I present here has little application—though a managerial approach of compassion and care is never harmful. In chronic trauma, the situation is more or less permanent, or at least predictably recurring.

In contrast, the traumas focused on in this book are *single-event* traumatic experiences, not chronic or long-standing ones. A TLE is precisely *one* traumatic experience, not a series of them or a persisting pattern of them. What I am calling a TLE is *a major single event whose traumatic effects temporarily limit the person's ability to act, respond, and perform naturally and normally*.

An Indirect TLE

As I mentioned, a person may be traumatized who was not the direct victim of the traumatic event. One manager in a large corporation told me that in one year, he had over a dozen traumatized parents who were affected not by something that had happened directly to them but by what had happened to their children. Here, in his own words, is how he described some of the traumas that affected employees in his workplace. *All the following stories of trauma come from one manager!*

"One of my fellow managers had a sixteen-year-old daughter who became pregnant by her same-age boyfriend; she was a brilliant high school student and her parents and teachers had planned a great college career for her. She got married instead. Her father is still not back to normal."

"Another mother was devastated when her son was arrested for armed robbery; she thinks it was all her fault for not bringing him up right."

"One of our secretaries had a daughter arrested for using and selling drugs; she had absolutely no idea what was going on, and she still walks around feeling guilty, shameful, and embarrassed."

"One man's son, a victim in an auto accident, was hospitalized for spinal cord injuries. It about killed him when the doctors said his son would never walk again—and the kid was a great baseball player."

"One of the nicest guys on our staff had a son who committed suicide; he's never been the same since and he keeps blaming himself."

"Another great guy had a daughter who had a nervous breakdown; she's going to lose at least one year of school in a mental hospital. The father might just as well be there himself; he can only do a fraction of the work he used to do for us."

"I've had parents whose kids were held up at gunpoint, whose apartments were broken into and robbed, who had children born with major birth defects or born dead. Parents of these kids walk around the shop with their heads hung down for weeks and months."

"Recently, I met with one of our managers, a father whose daughter had been raped. She was traumatized, but so was he. He went through periods of helplessness and rage—and it showed in his attitude at work. He felt inadequate as a parent because he was unable to protect her from the experience."

"The saddest example was one of our best technicians, a mother who was visiting her son in the hospital after a routine operation. By some error, the boy was given the wrong medication, he had an instant reaction to it, and he died within moments right in front of his mother. She has been under psychiatric care for months now."

"In the past year, I have had a number of employees who were also traumatized when something traumatic happened related to their spouse. One employee's spouse had a heart attack; another's committed suicide; another's was arrested for fraud and extortion; another's lost all the family savings gambling in Las Vegas; another's wrecked the car and killed someone while driving drunk; another's was diagnosed with pancreatic cancer and given only a few months to live; another's ran off abandoning her and taking all their money; another's ran off with their two young children."

These are just a sample of the single events that shock and traumatize people and change their lives, their self-image, their self-confidence, and their self-worth. The point is that TLEs are all around us. Not even counting those produced by violence in the workplace—shooting, hostage situations, suicides, arson, physical or sexual assault, acts of sabotage against equipment or property—there are countless other cases of TLEs. They have many physical and emotional consequences that employees bring with them as they return to work, trying to recover from their trauma.

These are the kinds of survivors that managers and coworkers can help.

CHAPTER THREE

~

What Is It Like to Be a Returning TLE Employee?

Reacting to Trauma

Edward, a fifty-five-year old bachelor, had been an employee of the US Postal Service for thirty-four years. During all these years he had lived with his mother, who recently died at the age of seventy-nine of a heart attack. His managers, knowing how close Edward was to his mother, told him to take a full week off. When Edward returned to his post office job, he found himself unable to get into his familiar efficient routine, even though he told his manager it felt good to be back among his fellow employees and it felt miserable being alone at home. However, during the day, amid all the hustle and bustle around him, Edward would sit at his desk and stare into space for long periods of time. One coworker heard him sobbing in the men's room. To fellow employees it seemed he always wanted to talk about his mother and to repeat stories about her that they had all heard before.

Ellemeta, a robust, strong-willed, middle-aged divorced woman who lived alone, worked in the same post office as Edward. Her trauma was being robbed in her home by a masked and armed intruder. He had come in through a window while she was asleep. As he held her at gunpoint, she went into shock, shaking in silence in her bed. He said he wanted only cash and jewelry. She obediently told him where he could find what he wanted. He had come and gone in less than five minutes, but those few minutes were burned into her memory. "My home was violated," she explained to a friend later on. "It was like being raped. To think I was *that* vulnerable." Although

Ellemeta reported the robbery to the police, there was little hope of catching him as he had been wearing a mask and gloves. They told her she was a "lucky" one and to think about putting iron bars on her windows. When she came back to work a few days later, she wasn't at all quiet and subdued like Edward. She ranted and raved. She was outraged and frustrated. She cursed the intruder with all the scathing remarks she could think of. She told co-workers what she should have done and would do if it happened again. She wouldn't be caught helpless and vulnerable the next time. She would get a gun, or she would move.

There is no such thing as a standard traumatized employee returning to the workplace, because no two people will react to a traumatic event in exactly the same way. Some, like Edward, will come back to work quiet, tentative, and hesitant. Others, like Ellemeta, will return angry, bitter, or even enraged. Still others will walk into the office feeling confused, frightened, and even ashamed.

Traumatic Limitations

What we do know is that, when a traumatized person returns to work, the effects generally *limit the person's ability to act, respond, perform, and make decisions naturally and normally*. Because of this, such survivors of trauma usually need a social readjustment period when they first return to the workplace. This readjustment period will certainly last much longer than one day and can sometimes stretch out into weeks, depending on the employee's personality and the severity and shock of the traumatic event.

Psychologists tell us that individuals that have never been traumatized before generally have an easier time in recovery. They are not as likely to be as devastated as those who have experienced multiple traumas in their lifetime, especially in childhood. In this sense, our emotional systems are like our muscular systems. If you have strained your back a number of times before now, you are more likely to strain it again when you try lifting something heavy than someone who has never had a strained back.

Wherever we have been emotionally wounded before we are more vulnerable there than in other areas where we have not been wounded. For example, two people can be in the same auto accident; one may be severely traumatized by the event with its effects lasting for months or years while the other person seems to bounce back to normal very quickly and is able to drive again without fear. Psychology says that the odds are that the first person had been traumatized before this, and that the second person had never been in a similar situation.

Personality Types Respond Differently

Of course, after a TLE, different personality types will react differently and process the event differently. Introverts like Edward, when they return to work after their experience, typically may not want to talk about the event. If you confront them about it, they often resist revealing their inner feelings. They will tend to stay focused on surface behavior, activities, and tasks. Like Edward, they may go to the restroom and cry alone.

In contrast, an extroverted returning traumatized employee, like Ellemeta, will need to talk about the experience and express feelings, unless those feelings are shameful or embarrassing, which they usually prefer to hide or camouflage.

Extroverts will sometimes tend to go to one or other emotional extreme when they return to work. They might appear either overconfident or utterly despondent. Consequently, in the period after their return they might require frequent renegotiation of workplace tasks and deadlines. Ellemeta, who usually waited on postal customers, was in no shape to deal with outside customers her first few days back, and she knew it. Her manager assigned her to work in the sorting room for the time being, where she could vent her emotions without affecting customers.

Trauma and Grief

Almost every TLE is also a traumatic *loss* experience. As such, part of the recovery from trauma involves some amount of grief work. Wherever there is loss, there will be grief. Edward's trauma involved losing a beloved human being. Ellemeta's trauma involved losing her sense of security. Others lose their jobs. Those who are betrayed lose their sense of trust in humanity. Some lose their self-respect. Others lose hope. In all cases, they must learn to grieve their particular loss. It is part of the trauma recovery process.

Grief is not a disease or an illness, according to William F. Doverspike, PhD, of the Georgia Psychological Association.

> Grief is not generally considered a disorder but rather is viewed as an adaptation to a loss. In this respect, the process of grieving is similar to the process of healing. It involves working through the stages of grief. The tasks of grieving include experiencing the pain of grief, accepting the reality of the loss, adjusting to an environment in which the loved one is missing, and withdrawing one's emotional energy and investing it in another relationship. Failure to complete these tasks can result in *impacted grief*, which is a prolonged type of grief associated with depression. Impacted grief can block further growth

and development. For example, the absence of family or social support during bereavement can complicate the process of grieving.

The resolution of grief requires accepting the reality of the loss, cognitively and emotionally, and reorganizing the facets of life in spite of the loss. However, it is not a return to the "old self." One never really returns to his or her former self. Instead one incorporates the experience into what eventually becomes a new self.[1]

Even Psychologists Can Be Traumatized

How do we distinguish loss from trauma and grief from loss? Any loss can be characterized as a trauma (divorce, car crash, career loss, financial loss, separation, and death).

Jamie Marich, PhD, in her book *Trauma Made Simple: Competencies in Assessment, Treatment and Working with Survivors* (2008), points out that we tend to use the terms *grief*, *bereavement*, and *mourning* interchangeably, although they have different meanings.

- *Grief* is the experience of loss in one's life.
- *Bereavement* is the state of living with and adapting to a loss.
- *Mourning* is the process of adaption to the loss.[2]

J. James Worden, a leader in the field in grief counseling and bereavement, slightly disagrees with his mentor George Engel on the semantics about mourning. Engel consistently uses the words *restoration* and *recovery* in his writing as the goal in the mourning process. Worden prefers the word *adaptation*—stating that some people may *adapt* better to grief or loss than others. Adaptation suggests that a person will never be the same after a loss. Both Worden and Engel agree that some people adapt better to grief and loss than others. The grief process is not the same for the any two people even if they are mourning the same loss.[3]

Physical Symptoms

In my own research, I found that physical health symptoms are generally the most obvious signs displayed by a returning traumatized employee. They include nausea, insomnia, headaches, lack of appetite, increased alcohol consumption, and fatigue. These symptoms are also likely to be the most disruptive in terms of the workplace. Sometimes, when these health problems resulting from the trauma manifest themselves after an employee has returned to work, the employee must take time off. These problems will certainly affect the level of productivity.

Since the publication of my first book, traumatic grief has now come into the conversation—so what is *traumatic grief?*

Traumatic grief is defined as grief stemming from a death or a traumatic distress (Jacobs, 1999). If people are grieving and experiencing separation anxiety, the symptoms will consist of yearning, searching. and loneliness. When there is concurrent traumatic distress, the person will also be experiencing numbness, disbelief, distrust, anger, and sense of futility about the future. Traumatic grief captures both dimensions of a person's response.

Recently, in her blog *When Grief Is Traumatic*, Virginia Hughes told the story of Vicki who lost her son in a motorcycle accident; he was pronounced brain dead at the hospital. Vicki was unable to cope at work for the next two years nor could she function well at home. She felt terribly guilty, she let her housework pile up and refused to see her friends. She just wanted to hold onto him—she turned his helmet into a flowerpot. Because she could not let go, she was unable to reconnect to her own life.[4]

Vicki represents 10 percent of grievers who have prolonged or traumatic grief lasting six months or more. They are grieving something very painful, feeling anger, a sense of loss, and being stuck. Researchers have tied prolonged traumatic grief to a host of symptoms such as sleep troubles and suicidal thoughts. Such grief may even lead to heart problems and cancer.

Holly Prigerson, director of the Center for Research on End of Life Care at Weill Cornell Medical College, has been involved with studying bereavement since the 1990s. She found from her research that prolonged traumatic grief seems to respond well to cognitive behavioral therapy (CBT), a talk therapy in which the patient identifies specific thoughts and feelings, ferrets out those that are not rational, and sets goals for the future. In 2005, Katherine Shear of Columbia University reported that a CBT tailored for complicated grief worked for 51 percent of patients.

After struggling for two years with a traditional therapist, Vicki saw a CBT therapist with whom she discussed her most vivid and painful memories of her son in the hospital. She remembered squeezing his hand and recalling all the emotions associated with him in the hospital. As she listened to herself telling her story, these recollections became less painful. Her level of anxiety dropped and she started to reach out to friends. She put aside her sympathy scrapbook. The CBT treatment led to a complete reframing of her son and their relationship.

She claimed that telling the story of his death was helpful in realizing that, though he had lived a dangerous life, he was an independent adult who made his own decisions. She was then able to move on with her own life and enjoy meeting her friends; the treatment worked.

Survivors of Job Loss

Loss can happen in many different ways for a person going through a trauma. At a certain time in my life, I was trying to start a consulting business on my own. It was very difficult, since both my husband and my mother were ill at the same time.

When my husband became very seriously ill, nurses from the local hospital reminded me of research showing that, after a husband dies, a wife will experience stress and illness. That warning alerted me that I should be aware of this and take care of myself.

Even though my husband had a private nurse, a professional companion, and round the clock caregivers as my helpers, shortly after he died in November 2010, I became very ill. I was diagnosed with sinusitis. I could not breathe properly. And along with that diagnosis, I developed a chronic cough that would not go away. It progressed for more than three months.

My doctor sent me for all types of tests. Even though the results came back "negative," I remained extremely weak and unable to function. I became petrified thinking that I had contacted a horrible, unrecognized disease. Our home is surrounded by woods. I felt that factor played an important role in the lack of a clear diagnosis. Gradually, after seeing a number of doctors, I began to get my strength back and started to feel normal.

At this same time, my mother was residing in a nursing home in the same town. She died in June 2012. With her death, I suffered a different kind of loss. It was one of loneliness and heartache. My therapist told me this death would be the hardest because "our mothers are with us the longest." She was right. I was totally lost after her death. Even though I give public lectures on loss, grief, and trauma, and have published a book on this issue, I personally had to deal with the deaths of two people I loved.

How did I resolve this loss? I talked to a therapist and I took a part-time job at a local retail store to keep me busy. It was the best thing that I could have done. The people at the store became my family and the experience of closeness and trust there was therapeutic for me. I created a new purpose in my life. Soon after I started to work at the store, I started to lecture again and write articles. Gradually, I began to regroup and reach out. I created a new network for myself.

Notes

1. William F. Doverspike, "Grief: The Journey from Suffering to Resilience," *Georgia Psychological Association* (2014): 1.

2. Jamie Marich, *Trauma Made Simple: Competencies in Assessment, Treatment and Working with Survivors*. Eau Claire, WI: PESI Publishing, 2014, 38.

3. Marich, *Trauma Made Simple*, 39.

4. Virginia Hughes, "When Grief Is Traumatic," *National Geographic*, November 7, 2014.

CHAPTER FOUR

~

What Can Managers Do?

The First Day Back to Work

If you are a manager, the odds are that in the last few months you probably had several employees who needed some days off because they had been through a TLE and were deeply emotionally affected by it.

What do you say to such people, like Edward and Ellemeta, when they first return to the workplace? What is the most appropriate way to treat such people when they come back? You realize you are not a professional counselor or therapist. You are not an employee assistance expert. You have not been trained in psychology, nor do you claim to understand the subtle working of the human psyche or the stages of understanding emotional recovery from a TLE. You're a manager.

You would like to do some good for the returning employee and yet you do not want to cause any emotional harm.

There are many ways to harm, or at least to hinder the emotional recovery process, even if you have the best intentions. Traumatized employees returning to the workplace for the first time have reported to me ways their managers and supervisors showed little or no sensitivity to the powerful emotional effects the TLE had on them.

Here are a few *don'ts* suggested by those traumatized employees whose experience upon return to the workplace was unhelpful. These are requests from employees to managers and supervisors.

- *Don't avoid us.*
- *Don't remain silent or aloof when we return to work.*
- *Don't act as if the trauma had never happened.*
- *Don't act as if everything is back to normal.*

  "My manager may have been unsure of the best way to welcome me back as an employee. He was afraid he would say the wrong thing," explained one survivor who remembered his first day back on the job. "The worst thing he did was to avoid me as if I had some contagious disease. I took his silence and avoidance as a clear message that he didn't really care about me or what happened to me, and that I didn't deserve his attention."

- *Don't start off talking to us about company problems and your problems.*

  "This happened to me," explained a woman about her first day back to work after her husband's heart attack. "My manager, who happens to be a woman, started in about how bad things were for her. She started listing all the problems she had at the office. She never asked about how I was feeling or how ready for work I was. I guess she simply wanted me to forget my traumatic experience—as if I could!—and expected me to go back to my desk as usual, as if nothing emotionally upsetting had ever happened."

  A much better approach would have been to tell the returning employee how important and valuable she was to the office staff and how much she was needed and appreciated. As it came out, the manager was communicating the message, "Look how bad my life is, too. You think you have problems? Just look at mine?"

- *Don't lay big expectations on us upon our return.*

  "My manager, the day I came back, told me that he had a big project waiting for me that he wanted me to take charge of," said one woman who had just returned from miscarrying a baby. "He told me that keeping me busy would take my mind off my 'situation.'"

If an employee returning to work after a trauma could say one thing to a manager, it would be something like this: "I need to feel safe and secure here in the workplace. I need to feel that you will protect me, respect my emotions, and make me feel welcome and cared about." Most returning employees couldn't formulate their needs that clearly, but it is what they most need and want.

They don't want to be coddled as a child, but they do want managers and their coworkers to respect them for surviving a powerfully negative emotional experience and may need time to recover from its effects.

A well-known manager who showed appropriate sensitivity to an employee going through a trauma was Mark Zuckerburg, the CEO of Facebook. He was the supervisor of Sheryl Sandberg, Facebook's COO, who lost her young husband Dave Goldberg to a sudden, fatal heart attack. What made it even more traumatic was that Dave died while celebrating his birthday with a group of friends at a resort in Mexico. Once she returned home, Mr. Zuckerburg extended his hand to Ms. Sandberg by giving her a compassionate "pep talk." He reminded her of her importance to the Facebook team, her need to take time off, and that she should have reasonable expectations of herself when returning to work.

That evening, Ms. Sandberg began journaling her thoughts. She stated, "Journaling became a key part of my recovery." In that journal she recorded everything, "from the smallest detail of my morning to the unanswerable questions of existence."[1]

What journaling did for Ms. Sandberg during her early period of grief was to help her gain her self-confidence back and slowly navigate her days in the workplace. She grew stronger in dealing with her coworkers and focused on what she called "small wins." This strategy motivated her on a daily basis to become aware of her behavior. As a result, her stress level was reduced.

Enter Compassionate Management

Since publishing my last book, the rise of *compassionate management* has finally come into the workplace. The *Harvard Business Review* published an article by Bronwyn Fryer that states that compassion concretely benefits the corporate line.

> First, compassion and curiosity increase employee loyalty and trust. Research has shown that feelings of warmth and positive relationships at work have a greater say over employee loyalty than the size of their paycheck. In particular, a study by Jonathan Haidt of New York University showed that the more employees look up to their leaders and are moved by their compassion or kindness (a state he terms "elevation"), the more loyal they become to him or her. So if you are more compassionate to your employee, not only will he or she be more loyal to you, but anyone else who has witnessed your behavior may also experience elevation and feel more devoted to you.[2]

Quoted in the *Harvard Business Review* article, LinkedIn CEO Jeff Weiner says,

> to manage compassionately, doesn't come naturally to most managers. It requires spending time to walk in someone's shoes—to understand what kind

of baggage that person is bringing to work; what kinds of stresses she's under; what her strengths and weaknesses are. In high-pressure environments, such a time investment is anathema to most of us.[3]

Weiner describes how such an investment is analogous to the work of a carpenter who carefully measures a piece of wood three times before cutting once. Spending such "compassion time" with an employee, Weiner insists, pays off in that person's much greater efficiency, productivity, and effectiveness (and obviates later regrets).

"It's not just altruism: as it turns out, companies that practice compassionate capitalism perform ten times better than companies that don't," said Weiner. He said that he was on a personal mission to "expand the world's collective wisdom and compassion," and that he had made "the practice of compassionate management a core value at the company."[4]

Eight Steps for the First Meeting

Here are first steps a manager should take as soon as traumatized employees return to work, even before they sit down at a desk or start to work.

1. *You, as manager, should initiate the first contact.* Do not wait for the employee to come to you. As soon as they arrive on their first day back to work, greet such employees with a quiet smile. Welcome them back. Tell them they have been missed. No need for backslapping or other overly enthusiastic greetings.

2. *Carry out your first dialogue privately in a quiet place.* Do it preferably in your office with the door closed. Ask a secretary to hold all phone calls. This tells the returning employees that you want to create a safe place for them. Remember, during these first few days, your main task is to help returning employees find their own level of comfort and security. Some may need much more reassurance than others. Let yourself be totally present to the employee as you talk. You should not appear distracted by reading mail or moving papers around on your desk.

3. *Be as composed as you can.* Gently look the returning employee in the eye. Don't avoid eye contact, but don't force it either. Some employees feel shame and embarrassment about their traumatic experiences. When the employee looks back at you, he or she should see someone who is calm and compassionate. The returning employee does not need to hear strong emotional responses from you. Your presence

should be supportive and responsive to their needs. Certainly, don't put pressure on the employee to get back to the job with phrases like, "Have we got a backlog work waiting for you!" or "You sure have a lot of catching up to do!"

4. *Be aware of possible fears the returning employees may have.* No need to quiz the employees to identify their fears. You can presume that fears are present. If at all possible, assure returning employees that their job is secure and waiting for them whenever they are ready to take it up again. Fears that returning TLE employees may have include:

- Fear that I will lose, or have already lost my old job.
- Fear that I am being, or have already been, replaced.
- Fear that the person who covered for me while I was gone did a better job than I ever did.
- Fear that, even if I have my job back, I won't be able to perform it as well as I used to.
- Fear that I won't be as fast or effective as I used to be.
- Fear that I won't have the physical strength to handle my job—or catch up.
- Fear that I will get emotionally upset and it will affect the quality of my work.
- Fear that the pressures of the job will now overwhelm me.
- Fear that I will make many mistakes because I get easily distracted these days.
- Fear that I can't meet deadlines.
- Fear that I will break down and cry during a meeting.
- Fear that my coworkers will have negative thoughts about me; for example, that I am a bad spouse or parent.
- Fear that my coworkers will pity me or feel sorry for me.
- Fear that my coworkers will laugh at me behind my back.
- Fear that my managers and coworkers will expect more than I can give right now.
- Fear that I may be seen as a weak person for needing time off.
- Fear that my coworkers will avoid me.
- Fear that my coworkers will try to pry into my personal life.

Of course, no returning employee will have all of these fears, but all TLE employees will have some of them or others like them. The traumatic experience has undermined their basic feelings of safety and security. They return to work feeling very vulnerable. Each of these fears may reflect some of that loss.

5. *Make certain that the employee is getting all possible professional help that the company provides.* Reassure returning employees that the company wants to help provide for their health. Among some people, there is still a sense of stigma or shame in seeing a psychologist or psychiatrist. Assure such employees that everyone encounters emotionally over-whelming times, and most people need psychological help in working through such stress. Such help is desirable and necessary for a healthy emotional recovery.

Make sure the employee is familiar with the Employee Assistance Program (EAP) and is receiving therapy or counseling, if it is needed or wanted by the employee. Many employees are unaware of an or-ganization's resources and how to access them. Whenever possible, you should facilitate the process, perhaps even walking with the employee to the EAP office or offering to help fill out complicated forms.

For your information, there are a number of consequences of trauma that may require professional help. Some of these signs in a returning TLE employee are:

- difficulty setting limits and boundaries with others
- a continuing sense of isolation
- strong feelings of worthlessness and powerlessness
- strong feelings of shame and guilt
- severe damage to self-esteem and self-image
- hypersensitivity and overreaction to normal situations
- suicidal gestures or attempts
- making threats of violence in the workplace
- making threats of physical harm to others
- depression or emotion deprivation
- addiction or substance abuse
- tendency to sabotage success
- tendency to be victimized by others

When you notice one or more of these symptoms in an employee returning to work after a traumatic life experience, especially if the symptoms persist beyond a few days, gently and compassionately check to see if the employee is under professional care. If not, see that appropriate care is found.

Neither you as a manager, nor your other employees, can be expected to deal with such symptoms and issues since they require professional help. Please do not attempt to play the role of psychotherapist with returning employees. Nor, in cases of violence in the workplace, are you expected to replace the security team or law enforcement. Your role, along with coworkers, is simply to provide an emotionally safe environment for the trauma survivors, to let them tell their story, if they wish, and to reestablish personal connections with the individuals.

6. *Conduct the interview in a nonthreatening way by asking only open-ended questions.* If you need to interact, ask very general questions, like:

- How can I be helpful?
- Do you need anything?
- Is there anything I can help you with? Doctor appointments? Schedules?
- Are you getting enough support at home?
- Do you have any questions about your reentry?
- Do you feel unsure or hesitant about anything?
- Is there anything specifically that you want or need today?
- How can I help you get what you need?
- What type of work do you feel up to?
- Do you feel comfortable going back to your regular desk?
- Is there anything you'd like me to say or not say to your coworkers?
- Is there anything you want to know from me?
- Is there anything you want me to know?
- Is there anything you want to talk to me about?

Trust that the returning employees know what they need. Don't presume that you know better than they what they need at the moment. That's why open-ended questions are the best. The way the employees answer your open-ended questions will provide the best leads for your response. The way the employees answer your open-ended questions will direct your conversation and tell you how to proceed.

7. *Establish a reentry program with the employee's cooperation and input.* Find out from the returning TLE employees how much they feel ready to attempt during the first few days. Together, set up a reentry plan

suggesting how much and how soon assignments can get done. Invite the employees to report, perhaps each day for the first week or so, how their reentry program is working. Clearly allow for such a program to be revised at the will of the employees. Don't presume you know what the employees can or cannot do at this time. In most cases, they themselves do not even know what they are capable of especially if the trauma was shocking. Remember, the employees need to feel secure in the workplace. If they are given more assignments than they can deal with, they will be emotionally overwhelmed and experience failure, which is not conducive to a safe and secure situation.

8. *Promise you will initiate regular contact with the returning employees. And keep your promise.* Invite the employees to come to see you whenever they wish to or feel a need to. If the employees do not initiate a visit within the next few days, you should suggest a meeting and find a quiet time and place for it. Ask some of the same open-ended questions provided earlier. They reinforce in the employee's mind that you intend to maintain a safe and secure environment. This is the best thing you can do to promote the emotional adjustment to their trauma.

In such future meetings, you may also ask about their worries, their difficulties readjusting, how adequately the company is caring for them, their own personal agendas, hopes, and dreams. In this way, if they wish, they may choose to share with you their trauma experience and what happened to them in some detail. A willingness to tell their story, especially if it is an embarrassing one, is a good sign that the survivors feel comfortable with you.

A Successful Reentry

Here is a story told to me by one of the managers who had attended a Dialogue Circle on the returning TLE employee.

Susan was one of the outgoing and caring people in our office. She was only in her early thirties, so we were all shocked and worried when we heard that, after a routine physical, she was diagnosed with breast cancer requiring a radical mastectomy. Needless to say it was traumatic for Susan herself, the diagnosis coming as a total surprise. An operation was scheduled within days. Susan called me, her manager, to let me know what had happened. Her usual cheerful voice was somber and strained with emotion. She didn't know exactly when she would be back to work. Maybe it would take a number of weeks.

She called again after the operation to say the doctors thought it was successful. "But you never know," she said.

I asked her if she would be willing to accept cards and phone calls from people in the office. She was agreeable to that, and said how she missed the people at work. "The doctors told me I'd be pretty tired after chemotherapy and radiation, but I guess I can talk on the phone." She said a number of the women from the office phoned and chatted with her from time to time, keeping her connected with people and events in the office.

One day, I had a phone call from Susan. "The doctors say I can start back to work next week as long as I take it easy. They don't want me to exhaust myself. If it's okay with you, I'd love to come back at least part time," she said. I noticed that she had that old sparkle in her voice again, so I assured her that she would be most welcome.

"I have a special favor to ask," she began. "You know that with chemotherapy, your hair falls out. I was no exception. Right now, I'm bald as an eagle. People have been telling me I should wear a wig, but you know me. I've never tried to hide anything. I'll wear bright scarves and various things to cover my head, but underneath I'll be bald. Do you think the gang at the office can tolerate a bald Susan in their midst?"

"What made you decide to take this approach?" I asked with genuine interest.

"Well," she said, "I'm doing it to remind me that I am a cancer survivor. I don't want to upset anybody in the office, but I also don't want to hide the fact of what I've been going through. I've finally realized there's nothing to be ashamed of about having cancer," she said. I complimented her on her courage and said I thought the office staff could handle her brightly covered head.

On the next day, I called the office staff together for a short meeting, told them that Susan would be coming back part time, that she was a courageous woman, and that she decided against hiding the fact that she had lost all her hair from chemotherapy. I told them what she had told me about being proud to be a cancer survivor, and how she didn't like to hide anything from those she considered her friends. I told them that Susan's cancer was a traumatic life experience, and while the doctors were working to help Susan heal her cancer, our job was to help her recover from the effects of her trauma. I reminded them that, to do this, we needed to create an emotional *welcome mat* for Susan in the office, and we should provide a *listening ear* to let her tell her story if she wished to, and that we should provide a *helping hand* to reconnect with her gently but lovingly.

I asked if anyone had any questions. Someone asked how we were supposed to make her feel safe. To my surprise, a number of people immediately volunteered suggestions about what they thought they could do. That triggered other ideas. In a short time, we felt we could provide a secure environment and we were all excited about welcoming Susan back.

On her first day back to work, Susan came directly to my office, as I had suggested to her over the phone the night before. She was wearing a bright red bandana over her head. We talked a bit how she felt coming back. She said she felt a bit anxious that the office staff would think she was weird because she came to work with a bald head. She feared that they would avoid her because she had cancer. Also she was afraid that she might find herself exhausted and tired out right in the middle of some meeting, which would embarrass her. I assured her that we were all ready for her. And we were.

After lunch, Susan came to my office, almost in tears, saying how great everyone had been to her and how all her fears about not being accepted had been groundless. "I even got compliments on my red bandana," she said.

Notes

1. Sheryl Sandberg and Adam Grant, *Option B: Facing Adversity, Building Resilience, and Finding Joy* (New York: Alfred A. Knopf, 2017), 67.

2. Bronwyn Fryer, "Compassion Management," *Harvard Business Review* (2013): 1–2.

3. Fryer, "Compassion Management," 2.

4. Fryer, "Compassion Management."

~

What to Tell Coworkers?

Helpful Coworkers

Even though you as a manager may have an understanding of the stages in trauma recovery and opportunities to strongly influence returning TLE employees, in the long run it is the coworkers who are likely to have more continual and closer contact with the returning employees than you. Therefore, they can be very helpful in promoting the reentry process for such employees. Together, you and the coworkers can assist returning employees by how you respond to them.

Like you, the returning employees' coworkers may be unsure of the most appropriate way to treat the returning survivors.

Like you, they may give unhelpful responses as well as helpful ones. It all depends on knowing the difference.

Like you, fellow employees, feeling less than competent and confident in dealing with trauma survivors, may want to avoid the returning employee and not mention the traumatic topic. In their hesitancy and anxiousness, they may prefer to act as though the traumatic experience had never happened and that everything is now perfectly normal—as if the employees had merely been absent for a few days with the flu. A lot of us are like that.

Avoidance and denial from coworkers are not helpful responses to returning employees who have had a TLE.

Although it would be better if most or many of the coworkers had received some educational instruction in a Dialogue Circle or workshop about the process of emotional recovery from trauma, you as their manager can give them a short course in the emotional recovery process plus a few simple but effective suggestions for facilitating the successful reentry of traumatized employees.

A Short Course in Trauma and Emotional Recovery

As a manager, you might say something to coworkers like the following:

> There are three important stages in a survivor's emotional recovery from trauma. We all need to be familiar with these stages because Sarah will be coming back to work tomorrow after her husband's death [insert the appropriate name and traumatic event] and we want to do all we can to assist in her recovery and reentry here. We can be very helpful.

1. *First, provide a welcome mat.* The first stage in emotional recovery is that the returning employee (Sarah, in this case) needs to feel safe and secure here at work. It is our job to create a welcoming atmosphere for her. People, like Sarah, returning to work, depending on the nature of their traumatic experience, may express different emotions. Sarah, having experienced the sudden loss of a loved one, might feel helpless or grieving. We might notice that during the day she is usually quiet or lost in her thoughts. Another person returning to work who had been robbed on the street may feel suspicious and afraid. We might notice that such a person appears jumpy and easily startled. A woman returning to us who had been raped may feel shameful, so she may want to avoid talking to us. A mother whose child was arrested for drugs may feel guilty. She may want to avoid talking to you as well. Employees returning after a stroke or heart attack or other illness may feel tired or weak. They may seem forgetful or unable to find their way around.

   So, any kind of teasing, name-calling, making demands, or criticizing are out of place. They make the survivor feel unsafe, insecure, and unwelcome. On the opposite side, if you avoid the employees or act as though they hadn't experienced a traumatic event, they will not feel safe or welcome either. For, by your silence you are, in effect, denying their reality. What is real is that they had a traumatic experience, and you need in some way to acknowledge that fact. Acknowledgment doesn't take very much effort. It is enough to say, "I'm sorry for your loss." Or "I heard what happened. That was terrible. I'm sorry. But I'm glad you're back."

2. *Next, provide a listening ear.* The second stage in emotional recovery involves allowing them, if they choose, to tell you about their traumatic experience. Much of the necessary work at this stage will happen between the survivors and a counselor or therapist. They are the ones who do the professional work. But all of us can still be helpful here. For example, if the returning employees want to tell you the story of what happened, let them tell you. But let them tell it to you in their own way, at their own speed, and in their own time. Don't probe. Don't try to force them to tell you the story and don't outright ask them to tell you all about it. That would make the situation emotionally unsafe for them. And we never want to make them feel unsafe or unwelcome. Rather, make a simple offer, especially if you are a good friend, and say, "If you ever need to talk about what happened, I'll be glad to listen." And leave it at that.

   It is not ever helpful to a returning TLE employee on the first day back—or even a week later—to confront the person by saying, "Tell me all about it. I want to hear everything." This might seem to the survivor more like a demand than an invitation. Such a demand would be an invasion of the person's inner feeling and immediately creates an unsafe place, for it is forcing the employee to talk about something that may be very personal and private. Honoring the person's privacy is a way of keeping her safe and protected.

3. *Next, lend a helping hand.* The third recovery stage for the emotional traumatized employees is their need to belong to the community they left. And we can help in that reconnection process. A traumatic life experience may have in many ways severed the survivors' connections with family, neighbors, and workplace colleagues. We may not think that anything has changed, but the traumatized employees do. The traumatic experience has changed Sarah, she does not see herself as the same person she was before the event. A short time ago, she saw herself as a married woman looking forward to a future with her husband. Now she must learn to see herself as a widow facing the future alone. Her very identity has been affected.

   Whether the traumatic event was as rape, a heart attack or, as in Sarah's case, the sudden loss of an immediate family member, it has changed the survivor's self-image. So, just as Sarah must find ways as a widow to reconnect to her family and neighbors, she also needs to get reconnected here at work in her new social status. And we can all help her do that. Not only does Sarah need us to create a safe place for her, she needs us to help her reconnect to us and to her job. Sarah may physically look the same to you when she returns, but inside she will probably feel different from the woman who left here a week ago. So, in some ways you may need to treat her as a "new" employee. Very gently. You may need to coach or help her a bit on her job. In other words, lend a helping hand. Don't expect her immediately to jump right back into her old groove. Don't be surprised if, for a time, she is a bit slower, a bit less effective than she used to be. She is dealing with much emotional distress and grief. Just reconnect with her gently.

Summary

To sum up, the three stages in the recovery process are:

1. *Put out a welcome mat.* Create a safe and secure workplace atmosphere for any employee returning after a TLE.
2. *Lend a listening ear.* Let survivors tell their story or trauma experience to you, but only if they need to want to.
3. *Offer a helping hand.* Help them get reconnected to you, to the other coworkers and to their jobs.

Some Suggestions

Here are some quick suggestions to give coworkers of returning TLE employees. Tell coworkers you too are following these suggestions, since they are the same for everyone.

Welcome the returning TLE employees warmly and compassionately. Make them feel safe in the work setting. Acknowledge their traumatic experience simply and very generally with something, such as "Welcome back, George. I was sorry to hear about your son's auto accident." Or, "Good to have you back, Helen. I heard what happened. I'm sorry." Or, "Mary, I'm sorry about what happened, but I'm glad to see you. Is there any way I can be helpful? If you have any questions, I'll be at my desk."

Remember that, even though trauma survivors may look fine on the outside, they are going through a lot of inner turmoil. Many of them feel confused or may have trouble concentrating. They may be easily frustrated or discouraged. They may have trouble staying focused on their work or seem to lack the energy for it. Some may feel anxiety and fear, others shame and guilt, or anger and frustration. They may not be sleeping well at night. They may feel nauseous. They may have lost their appetite. They may be bothered by headaches. They may start drinking. They are probably reexperiencing their traumatic event over and over in their imagination during the day. In themselves, these scary memories may lead to many distractions and a lack of the ability to concentrate. But they can no more choose to stop the images of their trauma from resurfacing than you could choose to stop yourself from a sudden sneeze; just be patient with them. Your job is always to create and maintain a safe environment for them.

Find simple ways to reestablish connections to you and to the workplace. They may not want to go out with the gang for lunch, but you might invite them to join you quietly for lunch or at one of the break times. Team up with them on their projects or yours. Affirm them each time they initiate or cooperate with an act of reconnection. "I noticed you and Phil working together this morning. He missed you and is really glad you're back." Or, "I noticed you were talking to Sally in the break room. I'm glad she's a friend of yours. She was worried about you while you were away."

Reconnecting before Returning to Work

Tom had been rushed to the hospital after a heart attack he suffered lifting his daughter's heavy suitcases into the truck of her car. It was after Thanksgiving dinner, and he was getting her ready for the drive back to college. He collapsed on the driveway. Soon the ambulance came. After a week in the hospital, he recuperated at home for another four weeks before his doctor allowed him to go back to work—but only on a part-time basis.

Tom's manager at work had been notified of the heart attack and hospitalization the day after it happened. He decided that he and Tom's coworkers should not get involved and should leave Tom alone during this time, to be with his wife and family. The manager thought he was doing the best thing for Tom, presuming Tom would be embarrassed for coworkers to see him in his weakened state. His assumption was very mistaken.

When Tom finally came back to work, he looked sad. He confided to one of his coworkers, "I never had a single card or phone call or visit from any of the guys and gals here at the shop. I really felt abandoned by everybody."

The manager could have helped Tom's adjustment of reentry very easily by contacting his wife and asking if Tom would welcome cards, phone calls, or visitors. If Tom or his wife had said that Tom *didn't* want any contact from the workplace that would have been a clear message. On the contrary, if Tom had wished to keep connected to his friends at work, they could have been fostering his recovery for all these weeks. They could have been supporting him by keeping him reconnected to the workplace community.

Even if Tom's response had been to refuse contact with coworkers—he may have felt too weak to cope with them at that moment—the manager could have suggested to Tom's wife that he or another employee be contacted if Tom changed his mind. Also, the manager could still call Tom's wife from time to time to let Tom know, through her, that he was thought of and cared about at the workplace.

Whenever a recuperating traumatized employee at home welcomes contact from coworkers, it is a healthy sign. A manager can pass on to fellow employees the survivor's wish for contact. In this way, forms of connection are not only welcome but also become a healing force. For an employee who remains connected to coworkers while hospitalized or at home, workplace reentry will be easier and more satisfying. But such contact should always be at the discretion of the traumatized employee.

Typical Questions Coworkers May Ask You

We live in an age where information on any subject is available on television, in books, or online. Despite all that availability, people tend to remain relatively uniformed, especially about psychological matters. Nevertheless, when they are confronted with a situation where they need information, most people are curious and will ask questions. As a manager, you will want to know how to answer some of their questions about trauma and emotional recovery. Here are a few of the most common.

What does an employee coming back to work for the first time feel like?
Most traumas involve an important loss. Some returning TLE employees may have lost a spouse, a child, a parent, a home, a job, a career, their physical security, their financial security, their social standing, their reputation, their honor, or their hopes. As a result, returning employees perceive *themselves* differently, even though they may look the same to you.

One woman may have been a happy and proud mother before her trauma, but returns to work as a childless mother or the mother of a criminal. Her "self" has a new—and unwelcome—meaning. Her inner identity, the way she sees herself, has changed.

A man may have been climbing the ladder of success in his company before his heart attack, but he returns to work realizing that the kinds of career promotion he had been looking forward to will probably not happen to him. His ladder has no more rungs on it.

What would a returning employee be afraid of?
There is no single answer to this question. It depends on a combination of factors including the nature and seriousness of the trauma as well as the

personality of the returning employee and his relationship with the manager and coworkers.

For example, if the person has been raped or their child has been arrested as a drug dealer, the returning employee may feel ashamed, defensive, guilty or embarrassed, and not want to face coworkers. They are afraid other employees may look at them as at fault, weak, ineffective, unworthy, or a failure. And so they fear the others will not want to associate with them or are saying negative things about them.

Other traumatic experiences, like being robbed or having one's car rammed into by a careless driver without insurance, may generate anger and frustration. Such returning employees may expect coworkers to be sympathetic and share their irate feelings. They might be afraid their coworkers will think they were to blame.

The returning TLE employees' personalities make a difference, too. With those who tend to hide their feelings, you may never know how they perceive themselves or what their needs are. Others who wear their hearts on their sleeves will usually tell you how they feel about themselves and indicate how they would like you to respond.

As you interact with a reentry employee, what is most important is not how they perceive themselves but how they perceive you perceiving them. They are hoping you will accept them and connect with them in their new "self." They are looking for understanding and support.

Here are some of the fears they have about how you will perceive them. These are some of the things they might be saying to themselves about you:

- I don't want him to see me get emotionally upset or break down and cry.
- I hope she doesn't think of me as a bad spouse or parent.
- What if my team partner avoids me?
- What if she tries to pry into my personal life?
- I couldn't stand it if any of my project team pitied me, felt sorry for me, or laughed at me behind my back.
- I'm afraid my manager will see me as a weak person for needing time off.

What does doing the job feel like for returning TLE employees? Do they find it hard to perform their jobs?

If the returning traumatized employee has been absent for only a few days, the readjustment to the job is usually easier than if the absence is much longer. The longer the person is away, the stranger it feels coming back to the workplace. It may be hard to get back into the routine and keep pace with everyone. They may fear not meeting your expectations of them.

"Jim came back to work the next day after his doctor told him he had prostate cancer," a phone company manager told me. "The news was pretty shocking, since it came right out of the blue. He was a bit distracted at his job for a few days after the news, but everybody on the team liked him and he knew it. I asked him if he wanted me to keep it quiet or inform his coworkers about the cancer. He said he would tell them himself in his own way. When he did, everyone was very supportive. Knowing that, he was able to work just fine from then on," he said.

If the workplace environment has always felt emotionally safe and inviting—creative assignments, enjoyable coworkers, an understanding manager, and job security—the reentry should go smoothly and easily, as it did for Jim. If the workplace had not been emotionally safe and inviting, the reentry may be more difficult.

Andrea was always a troublesome employee. Her manager knew it, her coworkers knew it, and she knew it. She was often on the edge of being fired. She complained a lot to anyone who would listen. It became harder and harder for people in the office to give her the benefit of the doubt. When her husband died suddenly, she remained away from the office for over three weeks. She said she had to get all his financial affairs in order and that he had kept very sloppy records. When she returned to the workplace, she had lots of fears about her place there. She felt quite insecure.

What are their fears about job security and job performance?
Just as returning employees may have fears about how others perceive them, they also have fears generated by their jobs and the workplace itself. For example, in thinking about job security and job performance, they may say to themselves things like:

- I'm afraid I will lose, or have already lost, my old job.
- I suspect I have already been replaced or they will feel they don't need me at all.
- I'm sure the person who covered for me while I was gone did a better job than I ever did.
- Even if I have my job back, maybe I won't be able to perform as well as I used to.
- Can I live up to expectations?
- Will I ever be as fast or effective as I used to be?
- Will I have the physical strength to handle my job—or catch up?

What are the hardest things for trauma survivors to face when returning to the workplace?

For the returning TLE employees the hardest things to face are the other employees and the job. They liked themselves better before the traumatic experience, and they feel sure you did too. That's why they're afraid to face you or they feel insecure about it.

Most traumatized employees believe they were more competent and capable before the trauma, and realize that it's quite obvious that their trauma has had a negative effect on their competency and capability.

Fred was outside the factory driving a forklift, minding his own business, when a fuel line broke and Fred was knocked off his forklift from the impact of the explosion. A few broken ribs and some severe burns put him into the hospital for several days. One long-term physical consequence of the accident for Fred was major hearing loss. Being able to hear well was an important part of Fred's job, so one of his biggest fears after returning to work was that he might be incapable of doing his job.

How long do the effects of trauma last?

It depends on the nature and severity of the traumatic experience. Obviously, the emotional consequences and other effects of a severe trauma such as a rape, a murder, a kidnapping, a hostage situation, or a robbery at gunpoint may last for months and years.

Isabel fell two stories down an open elevator shaft during its construction. Luckily, she wasn't killed by the fall. But the accident left her with long-term physical pain, dependency on pain-killing drugs, and a pervasive fear of construction areas and elevators. Whenever she hears construction equipment noises or stands in front of an elevator, the memory of her scary fall resurfaces.

Jerry is another example of the lasting effects of a single traumatic experience. One night, when everyone else had gone home from work and Jerry was the last to leave the building, he was mugged right outside the door to the parking lot. He was traumatized by the event. To this day, he is fearful and suspicious, jumpy and anxious in what used to be a nonthreatening environment. Nowadays, he is never the last one to leave the plant and often waits at quitting time inside the door for others so that he can walk to the parking lot as part of a group.

As another example, after lunch one day, Tanya was walking back to the office. Just as she was about to cross the street, a car turning the corner swerved and hit another car, which killed a pedestrian a few feet in front of her. Had she been at that curb a few seconds earlier, the dead pedestrian could have been her. Even though the accident did not happen to her—there was not a scratch on her body—she was traumatized by it. When she walked in the office door, her manager noticed that she looked unusually pale and called her over to talk. He realized that Tanya may have gone into shock, so he sent her to the nurse's office to rest and be cared for. He also told some of her coworkers that she had had a TLE and they should put out a welcome mat for her and let share what had happened to her. Many weeks later, coworkers still noticed how overcautious and fearful Tanya was crossing the street, even when they were walking with her.

As Phyllis Kosminsky comments in her book *Getting Back to Life When Grief Won't Heal*, we have a kind of thermostat that keeps us from taking in more than we can handle, a built-in mechanism that protects us from being overloaded by painful information.[1] That explains why mourning is generally a linear process. Most traumatized people may expect or even hope that they will feel better with each passing day. Instead, people tend to experience "waves" of grief; they shift back and forth between looking back and looking ahead, between immersion in sadness and periods of distance from their grief. This is a more normal way of moving onward in their life.

Is reentry different when the traumatic experience happens at the workplace than when it happens outside or at home?
Yes, very much so. If the traumatic experience happened at home, reminders of the trauma are more likely to be associated with the home environment, though some of the consequences will be felt in the workplace.

Traumas that happen on the job are different in that the workplace itself was the scene of the traumatic experience. So, every time the traumatized employees return to the workplace, it will remind them of their traumatic event.

Some of these workplace traumatic events may be "shared" experiences, such as a bomb threat, a rapist somewhere in the building (learning that someone was recently raped in the building), or an employee being confronted by a deranged or aggressive person.

"We had a shoot-out in our office," explained a technician. "Two people were killed, and a number of others were injured. I was one of those who got under my desk as soon as I heard the crazy guy shouting in the doorway. When it happened, I had just started my computer and my desktop screen had just come on. To this day, whenever I turn on my computer, I can hear that guy's voice screaming in anger. And instinctively I turn my head to see if anyone is in the doorway."

Another said, "Every time I take this green dress out of my closet to wear it to work, I remember it was the dress I wore the day we had the attacker in our office."

"How could I ever forget it? Look, here's a crack in my desk where a bullet hit. Every time I sit down, I am faced with that crack. If I hadn't been in the Ladies Room at the time, I would have taken that bullet instead of my desk."

"Natalie was my best friend, and she was shot to death by that crazy gunman. I keep her picture on my desk to remind me how lucky I am to be alive, and how sad I am that my best friend was killed for no reason at all," said a worker.

When a group of people have been traumatized by the same event, they tend to talk about it and revisit it more often. Many things in the workplace remind them of the trauma.

The office group who experienced the angry shooter got together and planted a tree near their building to commemorate those who died in the attack. They stood in a circle around the tree, holding hands. Someone offered a prayer that they might leave all their bad memories of the event outside the building. On the wall near the doorway they put photos of the two people who were shot to death, to honor their memory. It was their way of putting the negative effects of the traumatic incident behind them, so they could go forward with their work in peace.

Psychologists suggest that when a group of people who work together share a traumatic event, they need to ritualize what happened, so they can collectively get closure on the event.

Individually, they also may all need some form of professional psychological treatment for their trauma. Some may need it more than others. But, individual therapy does not replace the need for the employees as a group to ritualize the traumatic event and its consequences.

Do all people in a workplace react the same way to a trauma that happens there?
The answer is no. People will react differently depending on their past history of traumatic experience.

For example, five people on a special project team were seated around a conference table, everyone excitedly talking about a major delay confronting them. They wondered how they were going to deal with it and still make their project deadline within budget. Amid all this animated discussion, George, a key technician for the project, had a massive heart attack and died almost instantly, right there in front of the entire team.

Every team member had liked George. They had been working together daily as a team for over a year. No one, including George himself, had known he had a heart condition. Theoretically, every team member should have reacted to the TLE in the same way and to the same degree. But that did not happen.

Molly was the most seriously traumatized of the group. She had had a similar experience less than a year before, when her father, who was in the best of health, died instantly at the dining room table from an allergic reaction to some food. She had been traumatized by her father's death when it happened with all the family sitting and talking together. George's massive coronary was an almost exact replay of her earlier trauma.

Phil was the next most serious. Ten years ago, he had watched his brother die almost instantly on the street of a bullet wound in a drive-by shooting. George's death wasn't an exact replica of his brother's death, but it was close enough. In fact, he recalled, his brother's death was the first thought that came into his mind when he saw George collapse. Besides, Phil was sitting right next to George at the conference table when it happened.

Psychologists tell us that people with a history of similar traumatic experiences can be affected more powerfully by a similar traumatic experience than someone else might be who had not experienced a similar trauma before.

The others in the group had indeed gone through a TLE in watching George's death, but they were not seriously traumatized by it. Consequently, they needed less professional psychotherapeutic care than Molly and Phil. The project was put on hold for a few weeks, ostensibly until they could find a replacement for George, but in reality it was because the original project team members were emotionally unable to start up again so soon.

Their manager suggested they find a ritual that the team could carry out to bring closure to George's death for them. The team decided to meet once again in the room where George had died and to tell stories about George and the project. Finally, they each said a prayer aloud for George and told the group how they personally would remember him. They also decided informally to name the project after him. Even though it had its technical name, among themselves they called it "George's Project."

Note

1. Phyllis Kosminsky, *Getting Back to Life When Grief Won't Heal* (New York: McGraw-Hill, 2007), 41.

CHAPTER SIX

~

What Does Psychology
Tell Us about Trauma?

An Overview of Research

Returning employees who have been *severely* traumatized may need to see a professional psychotherapist. Usually, the Employee Assistance Counselor arranges this. Some traumatized persons may also need to be evaluated by a psychiatrist for medication to deal with emotional stress, since only physicians can write prescriptions.

It may be helpful for you as a manager of returning traumatized employees to have a general sense of what goes on psychologically when a person is traumatized, for example, such as with rape.

The Trauma of Rape

More than once a minute, 78 times an hour, 1,871 times a day, girls and women in America are raped, according to the latest statistics.[1] Rape also happens to men and boys, and it is also traumatic for them.

Rape is defined as sexual assault or abuse; sexual intercourse against the will and without the consent of the individual. Legally, rape is also a crime.

For most victims, rape is experienced primarily as an act of violence in which the sexual act is secondary to the brutality of the attack. Many rape cases are not reported by victims because of feelings of shame, embarrassment, or fear.

Most of all, rape produces a physical and psychological emergency—a TLE of the highest order—and the victim must be treated with compassion as well as professional competence.

Immediately after the crime of rape has occurred, victims should be calmed down as much as possible and assured that they are safe.[2] Bleeding wounds, fractures, and other existing injuries should be treated with first aid. If victims refuse to seek medical, legal, or psychological help, they have a right to make such a choice, but they should be encouraged to consult a physician as soon as possible. If victims decide to report the crime, they are advised not to change clothes, bathe, douche, or urinate because these actions may destroy legal evidence needed to arrest and convict the attacker.[3]

Psychological recovery from rape is a difficult task. Some victims may appear to return to normal rather quickly, yet they are actually using temporary psychological mechanisms such as denial, suppression, and rationalization to mask the effects of trauma. Foa and Rothbaum in their book *Treating the Trauma of Rape: Cognitive-Behavioral Therapy for PTSD* suggest that victims may still be in shock up to two weeks after the traumatic event.[4]

Crisis intervention through all phases of the emotional recovery period has always been seen as a necessary component of the total professional care of a rape victim. However, Foa and Rothbaum report that, to date, there is no well-researched evidence that commonly used crisis interventions have proven effective. Rather, they suggest that trauma victims are better able to benefit from *interventions that process the event later on rather than immediately following the trauma*, especially if the victims are still in shock.

Emotionally, the main purposes of professional follow-ups are to keep the channels of communication open to the victims, to find out how they are doing, to offer support and encouragement in their efforts to resume life, and to provide assistance and referral if necessary.[5] Above all, it is imperative that healthcare professionals avoid any tendency to moralize or sit in judgment of the victim.

This advice is also well taken for managers and coworkers upon the return to the workplace of a rape survivor. Be compassionate, provide an emotional safe place, and keep channels of communication open. Simply say you know what happened and are very sorry about it. Do not ask for details of the trauma, as the memory of it may, for some time, generate shame, embarrassment, guilt, or fear. Above all, avoid any tendency to moralize or sit in judgment of the employee. For managers or coworkers to suggest or even infer that the victims might have "invited" the rape or "agreed" to it would only exacerbate the trauma's already deleterious effects and hinder recovery.

Most survivors of trauma relive their traumatic experiences over and over again in flashes of memory. They cannot seem to stop themselves from doing it. Unfortunately, this often causes additional stress in their lives and can even create a more permanent psychological disorder.

Posttraumatic Stress Disorder

Many psychotherapeutic techniques have been developed and tried in hopes of reducing the kinds of interruptive flashbacks and other emotional debilitation that traumatized people suffer. Most of these techniques have been studied with traumas that qualify as PTSD. Much of this research began in earnest after the Vietnam conflict when many veterans who had been in or near violent combat showed the symptoms of PTSD.[6]

PTSD is described in the *Diagnostic and Statistical Manual of Mental Disorders*, published by the American Psychiatric Association as an anxiety disorder precipitated by an event (trauma) that falls outside usual human experience and characterized by symptoms of *re-experiencing* (e.g., nightmares, flashback), *avoidance and numbing* (e.g., avoidance of reminders, selective amnesia), and *arousal* (e.g., difficulty sleeping, exaggerated startle) that persist longer than one month after the trauma.[7] (PTSD affects close to 50 percent of women who have been raped.[8] In fact, in one study, 76 percent of rape victims report PTSD symptoms at some point within a year after the assault.)[9]

After any major trauma, almost all people will experience psychological disturbance. This is normal and most will recover over time, so it is important to distinguish between a normal reaction to trauma and a pathological one that qualifies as PTSD and requires special intervention. For example, the small percentage of rape victims who do not qualify as PTSD are usually diagnosed as falling into a relatively new psychiatric category called *acute stress disorder*.[10] The major difference between these two psychiatric categories is not their symptoms but their duration. When symptoms persist beyond one month, a diagnosis of PTSD is appropriate.

For example, ten years after the war, PTSD veterans were still having flashbacks of battle. They might be sitting with a group of friends at a picnic, hear a car backfire or a firecracker go off, and in their minds and imaginations they are back in Vietnam. They are reliving the episode as if it were still happening at this moment. Their bodies cringe in fear. Because the trauma repeatedly and unpredictably interrupts them, even amid daily activities, many could not resume the normal course of their lives. For some, "it's as if time had stopped at the moment of the trauma."[11]

With the rise of the women's movement in the 1960s, therapists began to notice that rape victims and women living in severe abusive situations also manifested PTSD symptoms. Only in the 1970s, when Judith Lewis Herman wrote *Trauma and Recovery* was it "recognized that the most common post-traumatic disorders are those not of men in war but of women in civilian life."[12] But it was only in the next decade that psychologists and the courts recognized that traumatic events like rape and other violent acts were not simply single events, but experiences that produced extended physical, mental, and emotional consequences in the victim. Survivors reported bouts of insomnia, nausea, nightmares, dissociation, numbness, and startle responses for weeks and months after the traumatic experience.

One rape survivor wrote, "I was terrified to go anywhere on my own. . . . I felt too defenseless and too afraid, and so I just stopped doing anything. . . . I would just stay home and I was just frightened."[13]

Today, a much wider spectrum of traumatic experiences are being classified as PTSD—people witnessing a cruel murder firsthand, people involved in major accidents, people held hostage, people affected by an explosion or trapped in a burning building, or people witnessing the sudden death of a loved one when it was not anticipated. All of these survivors manifest many of the physical, mental, and emotional consequences of military combat trauma or rape as well as a memory processing system that was short-circuited.

The Way Memory Works

Normally, when events occur in our lives, whether they are important or unimportant, a number of standard steps are taken automatically in our brains, where memories are processed and stored. Typically, when an event first occurs, it is registered as an "episode" of sensory and emotional details in the limbic system of the brain, specifically in a certain area of the hippocampus.[14] An episodic memory is as yet unconnected and unassociated with the rest of our lives or our activities. Think of an episodic memory as a package dropped at your doorstep by a delivery person. You don't yet know who it is for or where it will be placed in your house. At this point, it is just an incomplete process—a package on your doorstep. The package needs to be opened, identified, and given meaning. The same needs to happen to any event that is held only in its episodic form in your limbic brain. At that point, it is merely a bundle of sensations and feelings just waiting at the brain's memory doorstep.

Normally, according to van der Kolk, details of the episodic memory are carried almost immediately from the hippocampus to the prefrontal area of your neocortex, the thinking part of your brain, somewhere behind your eyes.[15] There, the sensory and emotional details from the event are extracted, abstracted, and formed into a story. The event is given meaning, significance, and even an ethical perspective for you. The memory gets logged in, as it were, with a date and time stamped on it; it becomes a part of your history. It is put into its temporal-spatial context. There, at the same time it is also associated with other things that are currently happening—the clothes you are wearing, the others who are present, and so on—to form a fuller story.[16]

Technically, in this cerebral location, the episodic memory is given what brain researchers call a "semantic meaning," and, in moments, it is sent back to another area of the hippocampus to be stored as a regular memory, able to be recalled when needed.[17] This is what happens with the memory of a *normal* event.[18]

For example, if I attend a concert and have a great time, I remember not only the concert, but also all the details surrounding the event—what I was wearing, who was with me, what we had to eat and drink, what we did afterward. My brain gives the event a semantic meaning and locates it in my history. From then on, I can remember the date and time when it happened, and I can look back upon it and locate it among other events in my life.

Some memories are of special importance to us. For example, if you ask people where they were at the time of President Kennedy's assassination or when the space shuttle Challenger exploded or when the World Trade Center was blown up, most people can remember. This means these are very important semantic memories.

Short-Circuited Memory Process

According to Bergmann something different happens—or rather *doesn't* happen—when a traumatic event occurs.[19] Immediately after the traumatic experience, we observe that the traumatized person may go into shock. Such persons may feel stunned, startled, helpless, and defenseless to fight off or flee from the overwhelming event. They are often disoriented. When you ask them later, what they did or said immediately after the traumatic event, they often cannot remember.

Brain researchers tell us that in cases like these, the normal memory cycle in the brain gets short-circuited. The event is registered as an episodic memory. Your brain has completed the first step in the memory cycle, but the process stops there. Such traumatic events never get their semantic meanings. Traumatic events, especially powerful ones, never get beyond episodic memory. This means the traumatic event is not tied to any time and place in the person's history; it has no context in the survivor's life. So, the episodic traumatic memory can burst out and replay itself randomly over and over as if it were always happening for the first time.

When an episodic memory replays itself, it seems real and immediate, even though, in fact, it may have happened weeks, months, or even years ago. Such spontaneous recurrences of the traumatic episode are called "flash-backs." When these replays happen during ordinary activities, such as at work, they disorient the person having them, for they reactivate the trauma. It is usually quite obvious when a person is having a flashback in a workplace setting such as at meetings or when a team is together, because the trauma survivor may go blank or may be unsuspectingly flooded with images of the trauma and emotions associated with it. The survivor apparently has little power to stop these images and emotions and is overwhelmed once again by an event that happened in the past.

Solving an Old Dilemma

This short-circuited memory processing that happens in trauma has been recognized for more than a century. In 1889, the French physician Pierre Janet wrote a major work on psychological trauma. Using careful research, including hypnosis, Janet showed that traumatic memories were preserved in "an abnormal state, set apart from ordinary consciousness."[20] He believed that the intense emotional reaction to traumatic experiences severed the normal connection of memory, knowledge, and emotion. Such intense emotion, he wrote, incapacitated the synthesizing function of the mind.[21]

Janet had to come to these insightful conclusions through inference, for he had no way of looking at the brain directly or watching its activity as we do today. It is only in our era of highly sophisticated methods of brain scanning that we can light up different parts of the brain, so to speak, and verify these cerebral locations, pathways, and processes—and recognize the way trauma incapacitates the synthesizing function of the mind.[22]

Making a Traumatic Memory a Normal Memory

The best hope for full recovery and psychological healing from trauma seems to happen only after the episodic memory, stuck in one area of the hippocampus, can complete its natural cycle, be given semantic meaning in the prefrontal cortex, and be returned to another area of the hippocampus as a normal memory. Once a traumatic event completes the normal memory cycle, the person can recall the event without reexperiencing it with all its overwhelming emotion. Such a person can remember that the event happened in their personal history at a certain time and place, and belongs in the past. They know, for the first time perhaps, that the trauma is not happening now.

Categories of Intervention

There are three general categories of intervention for PTSD in general and other traumatic life experiences.

The first category is *psychosocial*. It includes: (1) hypnotherapy, (2) psychodynamic psychotherapy, and (3) group therapy. Since at least the time of Freud, hypnosis has continued to be used in treating trauma victims in order to resolve the psychic conflict.[23] Dynamic psychotherapists in treating traumatized victims emphasize concepts such as denial, abreaction, and catharsis, and have outlined stages of recovery from trauma;[24] however, psychoanalytically oriented therapy has not proven very successful.[25] Apparently, these approaches, especially with clients with PTSD symptoms, are not generally effective in transforming the episodic memory of the trauma into a normal memory.

Other psychodynamic approaches focus primarily on group process but they have not been widely tested.[26] PTSD combat veterans discovered that getting together in group therapy sessions, telling one another their trauma stories, seemed to be more helpful than one-on-one classical psychotherapy.

Managers and coworkers can encourage returning TLE employees to take advantage of whatever professional help they can get, and to stay with it, even though it doesn't seem to be immediately helpful. If there are informal support groups available—and there usually are, from cancer survivor support groups to pet loss support groups—encourage trauma survivors to participate in them. Many people find them comforting, supportive, and healing.

The second category is *pharmacological intervention*. Medication has been used for more than one hundred years to alleviate distress following trauma. Currently, these approaches to the trauma of rape advocate the use of medications either (1) to *reactivate* the traumatic experience as a means to help uncover repressed or dissociated material or, in complete contrast, (2) to *suppress* symptoms that are disrupting victims' lives, allowing them to restore their normal effective coping mechanisms.[27] (Using medication with traumatized persons is based on the evidence that traumatic events leave their imprint on the victim's limbic brain circuitry, autonomic nervous system, and arousal systems, and that drugs can help restore proper brain and memory functioning. The return to medication is also in response to the research showing that traditional psychotherapy has little or no effect in reestablishing normalcy after such imprinting.)[28]

Managers and coworkers should be aware that many pharmaceutical drug interventions for trauma victims can have an effect on the returning TLE employees' abilities to perform certain jobs. For example, many medications today have warning labels, advising that persons while under the drug's influence should not drive a car or operate dangerous machinery. When a returning employee has such a job, you might ask: "Do you happen to be taking any medications that are meant to calm and relax you? If so, I don't want you to be in any danger of getting hurt. Perhaps, we can shift some of your responsibilities for a while?"

Cognitive-Behavioral Approaches

The third category, the most rigorously researched, are the *cognitive-behavioral* approaches. Among this category are one set of approaches called *anxiety management training* (AMT), which includes techniques such as (1) stress inoculation training, (2) thought-stopping, and (3) cognitive restructuring.[29] These techniques to foster recovery from trauma are based on the belief that the victims feel pathological anxiety because they are deficient in personal coping skills.[30] AMT techniques include relaxation training, positive self-statements, breathing retraining, biofeedback, social skills training, and distraction methods. The aim of AMT is to furnish clients with ways to manage anxiety when it occurs. They are akin to the pharmacological approaches that use medication to suppress disruptive symptoms following the trauma.

Another set of approaches in this cognitive-behavioral category are called *exposure techniques* such as (1) systematic desensitization, (2) other imaginal and *in vivo* exposure treatments such as prolonged exposure, and (3) eye movement desensitization and reprocessing (EMDR). In contrast to AMT techniques whose purpose is to reduce anxiety and take the client's mind off the traumatic event, these approaches take an opposite tack and seek to activate traumatic memories—much as the reactivating pharmacological approaches attempt to do. Their underlying assumption is that by exposing and confronting the feared situation they can help the victim modify pathological aspects of these memories. According to Foa and Rothbaum, exposure techniques have proven to be the most effective, the most efficient, and the most user-friendly.[31]

In *systematic desensitization*, the therapist uses pairs of short events (an image of the fearful experience combined with relaxation) in a graded sequence beginning with the least distressing scenario. Thus, systematically, the client confronts scenarios that are more and more frightening, culminating in dealing with an imaginal image of the original trauma.[32]

Other *imaginal exposure treatments* found that pairing "relaxation" with the fearful stimuli, as was done in the systematic desensitization approach, was unnecessary. Instead, they use a variety of imaginal and *in vivo* (real life) exposure techniques, which promote the experience of anxiety during confrontation with the feared situation or image.[33] In this approach, the therapist might show the survivor photographs of the trauma setting—for example, the place where the rape was initiated—and eventually accompany the survivor to the physical location itself. Prolonged exposure is one of these techniques. Its program begins with breathing retraining, and then focuses on exposing the client in reality (*in vivo*) to the feared situation plus repeated reliving of the trauma in imagination. In their book, *Treating the Trauma of Rape*, Foa and Rothbaum find prolonged exposure to be the treatment of choice for rape victims who meet PTSD criteria. Other approaches or various combinations of treatments that favor desensitization of the memory have been tried.

Again, managers and coworkers should encourage returning TLE employees to take advantage of any professional help that is readily available, and to keep using it as long as it proves helpful.

Eye Movement Desensitization and Reprocessing

More recently, a rather easy technique of bilateral simulation of the brain while the survivor is recalling the traumatic event seems able, simply and directly, to help the brain complete the normal memory process. The process is called eye movement desensitization and reprocessing, or EMDR.[34] Apparently, such bilateral stimulation allows the brain to take the episodic memory up to the cortex, give it a semantic meaning there, and return it to the hippocampus as a normal memory.[35] After successful EMDR, the traumatic event is stored like any other memory, in its historical context. And the flashbacks disappear.

Originally, this bilateral stimulation was done by the therapist waving a finger back and forth in front of the client's eyes, asking the client to track the finger movement with her eyes. Thus the name "eye movement" desensitization. Today, the bilateral brain stimulation may be accomplished using a variety of modes, for example, by alternately tapping the client's left and right shoulders.[36] The bilateral stimulation process is repeated until anxiety decreases.

An EMDR treatment does not end merely with a reduction of anxiety. Its bilateral stimulation may also be used to help victims come to a realistically positive view of themselves. Instead of still seeing themselves as either dirty, guilty, shameful, damaged, or bad, they are encouraged to view themselves as survivors, as persons who are courageous, resourceful, and strong. This EMDR process is referred to as "installing a positive cognition."[37]

Managers and coworkers can support any returning TLE employees who are seeking EMDR. Those certified to do EMDR are almost always people licensed in a mental health profession.

Healing Trauma Using the Body's Sensations

While most therapists traditionally regard posttraumatic stress as a disorder of the mind and use mental or mind-altering pharmaceuticals to treat it, there are others who claim that trauma can be healed only by treatment that integrates body and mind. While talk therapy and drugs can be helpful, Peter A. Levine writes, in *Waking the Tiger: Healing Trauma*, "Trauma is not, will not, and can never be fully healed until we also address the essential role played by the body. We must understand how the body is affected by trauma and its central position in its aftermath."[38]

This approach is based on the fact that the body itself reacts profoundly to a traumatic experience. Just as the mind protects itself from being overwhelmed, so does the body. For example, the body may tense its muscles, shake in fear, freeze in terror, or collapse and shut itself off when overwhelmed. Just as mental treatments are designed to normalize the mind's activity after the event, the body's responses are meant to be normalized after the event, and if this somatic process goes unrecognized and untreated, the trauma can never be fully healed. "Somatic experiencing" is a well-integrated body-mind process developed by Peter Levine and based on the "felt sense" concept coined by Eugene Gendlin in his 1978 book *Focusing*. In these body-centered approaches, "Body sensation, rather than intense emotion, is the key to healing trauma," claims Levine.[39] However, these approaches are relatively new and have not been the subject of much scientific research. Nevertheless, they will undoubtedly become more recognized.

Since the first edition of my book, researchers, armed with brain-imaging machines and techniques of analysis, have provided scientists and doctors with significant and sophisticated understanding about the way the brain processes experience and information. That new research has enabled practitioners to better understand the damage inflicted by trauma and has enabled them to formulate new skills for repairing that damage. For a comprehensive survey of the most recent brain-mind-body research and its application to current trauma treatment approaches, see Bessel van der Kolk, MD, *The Body Keeps the Score: Brain, Mind, and Body in the Healing of Trauma*, published in 2015.[40]

A Word to Managers

The suggestions given to managers and coworkers in dealing with return-ing TLE employees do not in themselves change the episodic memory to a normal one, heal the trauma, or remove its unwelcomed physical con-sequences. These three simple recommendations do provide an important *context* for the emotional recovery process to take place. In other words, what managers and coworkers can do does not replace any necessary pro-fessional therapeutic work, but they can make a significant contribution. In quick review:

Put out a welcome mat. Since the TLE employees feel unsure, insecure, anxious, and upset after the traumatic event, managers and coworkers cre-ating a safe context in the workplace for the returning employee provide a necessary context for successful and timely recovery. The fact is that a thera-pist can create safe context for the survivor only for the length of a therapy session. In contrast, managers and coworkers can create a safe place for the length of a workday, every workday.

Lend a listening ear. Since the traumatic event itself remains prominent in the survivor's consciousness while the emotional recovery process is taking place, managers and coworkers remain open to the survivor's retelling of the trauma story. This willingness to listen may offer temporary relief to the sometimes confused and dissociated employee.

Offer a helping hand. Traumatic events themselves change the persons who undergo them, so that former personal connections and relationships feel lost or broken. Therefore, managers and coworkers who help restore connections between the returning TLE employee and the workplace are cooperating in the emotional recovery process in a way that a therapist or a therapy group cannot do. The therapist cannot reestablish the patient's mental and emotional connections with significant people in the patient's life. Only the patient and those significant people can do that. For most people, especially traumatized employees, their workplace is a major source of community. Reestablishing connections with managers and fellow workers is something only those employees can facilitate. And it is often they who must initiate the helping hand.

Notes

1. J. A. Bates. "Is the Silence Broken? Thirty Years after Rape Crisis Centers," Healtheon: *WebMD Medical News*, 2000.

2. Bates, "Is the Silence Broken?"

3. *Miller-Keane Medical Dictionary* (Healtheon: WebMD Medical News, 2000).

4. E. B. Foa and B. O. Rothbaum, *Treating the Trauma of Rape: Cognitive-Behavioral Therapy for PTSD* (New York: Guilford Press, 1998).

5. Miller-Keane, *Miller-Keane Medical Dictionary*.

6. The first formal recognition of PTSD as an official diagnosis did not occur in the American Psychiatric Association's manual of mental disorders (DSM-III-R) until 1980.

7. American Psychiatric Association, *Diagnostic and Statistical Manual of Mental Disorders*, 5th ed. (Washington, DC: APA, 2013).

8. B. O. Rothbaum, E. B. Foa, D. Riggs, T. Murdock, and W. W. Walsh, "A Prospective Examination of Post-Traumatic Stress Disorder in Rape Victims," *Journal of Traumatic Stress* 5 (1992): 455–75.

9. H. Resnick, L. J. Veronen, B. Saunders, D. G. Kilpatrick, and V. Cornelison, "Assessment of PTSD in a Subset of Rape Victims at 12 to 36 Months Post-Assault." Unpublished manuscript, 1998, reported in Foa and Rothbaum, *Treating the Trauma of Rape*.

10. American Psychiatric Association, *Diagnostic and Statistical Manual of Mental Disorders*, 4th ed. (Washington, DC: APA 1994).

11. Judith Lewis Herman, *Trauma and Recovery: The Aftermath of Violence—From Domestic Abuse to Political Terror* (New York: Basic Books, 1992), 37.

12. Herman, *Trauma and Recovery*, 28.

13. N. Connell and C. Wilson, editors, *Rape: The First Sourcebook for Women* (New York: New American Library, 1974), 44.

14. A. Schore, "Traumatic Attachment and the Development of the Right Brain." Paper given at the EMDR International Conference, Toronto, Ontario, 2000.

15. B. A. van der Kolk, M. S. Greenberg, H. Boyd, H., and J. Krystal, J. "Inescapable Shock, Neurotransmitters and Addiction to Trauma: Towards a Psychobiology of Post-Traumatic Stress," *Biological Psychiatry* 20 (1985): 314–25.

16. B. A. van der Kolk, M. S. Green, H. Boyd, and J. Krystal, "Inescapable Shock, Neurotransmitters and Addiction to Trauma: Towards a Psychobiology of Post-Traumatic," *Biological Psychiatry* 20 (1985): 314–25.

17. U. Bergmann, "Exploring the Role of the Cerebellum in EMDR Processing." Paper given at the EMDR International Conference, Toronto, Ontario, 2000.

18. Many other parts of the brain, such as the amygdala, medulla, pons, and cerebellum as well as many chemical neurotransmitters, are involved in the brain's complex system for processing memories, but for our purposes this simplified version is enough.

19. Bergmann, "Exploring the Role of the Cerebellum in EMDR Processing."

20. B. A. van der Kolk and O. van der Hart, "The Intrusive Past: The Flexibility of Memory and the Engraving of Trauma," *Imago* 48 (1991): 425.

21. Pierre Janet, *L'Automatisme Psychologique* (Paris: Felix Alcan, 1889), 457. Janet's research was mainly with women traumatized by rape and incest.

22. Fifty years after Janet, working with victims of combat trauma after World War II, Abraham Kardiner came to much the same conclusion.

23. D. Spiegel, "Hypnosis in the Treatment of Victims of Sexual Abuse," *Psychiatric Clinics of North America* 12(2) (1989): 295–305.

24. M. J. Horowitz, *Stress Response Syndromes*, 2nd ed. (Northvale, NJ: Jason Aronson, 1986).

25. P. Bart, "Unalienating Abortion, Demystifying Depression, and Restoring Rape Victims." Paper presented at the 128th Annual convention of the American Psychiatric Association, Anaheim, CA, 1975.

26. I. Yalom, *The Theory and Practice of Group Psychotherapy*, 4th ed. (New York: Basic Books, 1995).

27. W. W. Sargent and E. Slater, "Acute War Neuroses," *Lancet* (1940): ii, 1–2.

28. P. ver Ellen and D. P. Kammen, "The Biological Findings in Post-Traumatic Stress Disorder: A Review," *Journal of Applied Social Psychology* 20(21) (1990): 1789–1821.

29. E. B. Foa and B. O. Rothbaum, *Treating the Trauma of Rape: Cognitive-Behavioral Therapy for PTSD* (New York: Guilford Press, 1998).

30. R. Suinn, "Anxiety Management Training for General Anxiety," in *The Innovative Therapy: Critical and Creative Contributions*, R. Suinn and R. Wiegel, eds. (New York: Harper & Row, 1974).

31. Foa and Rothbaum, *Treating the Trauma of Rape*.

32. J. B. Frank, T. R. Kosten, E. I. Giller, and E. Dan, E. "A Randomized Clinical Trial of Phenelzine and Phenelzine and Imipramine for Post-Traumatic Stress Disorder," *American Journal of Psychiatry* 145 (1988): 1289–91.

33. C. H. John, J. D. Gilmore, and R. Z. Shenoy, "Use of a Feeding Procedure in the Treatment of a Stress-Related Anxiety Disorder," *Journal of Behavior Therapy and Experimental Psychiatry* 13 (1982): 235–37.

34. F. Shapiro, *Eye Movement Desensitization and Reprocessing: Basis Principles, Protocols, and Procedures* (New York: Guilford Press, 1995).

35. van der Kolk et al., "Inescapable Shock"; Schore, "Traumatic Attachment and the Development of the Right Brain."

36. L. Parnell, *Transforming Trauma: EMDR* (New York: Norton, 1997).

37. Parnell, *Transforming Trauma*.

38. Peter A. Levine, *Waking the Tiger: Healing Trauma* (Berkeley, CA: North Atlantic Books, 1997), 3.

39. Eugene Gendlin, *Focusing* (New York: Bantam Books, 1978), 10.

40. Bessel van der Kolk, *The Body Keeps the Score: Brain, Mind, and Body in the Healing of Trauma* (New York: Penguin Books, 2015).

CHAPTER SEVEN

~

What Can an Employee Assistance Program Do?

What Is an Employee Assistance Program?

Everyone knows that when people feel good they tend to work well. Unfortunately, there are things that occur that can traumatize employees. Some of these deeply upsetting experiences happen on the job, but many don't have anything to do with the workplace. Regardless of what can traumatize an employee, the negative feelings—fear, confusion, embarrassment, anger, distrust, shame, irritability, anxiety, worries—of one person can easily affect an entire work group. And this is where an Employee Assistance Program (EAP) comes in, for it can help employees resolve certain problems.

Most government agencies and large companies have an EAP with counselors, to whom managers may refer employees who have had TLEs. Managers ensure that such employees see a counselor.

However, since most employees have not used EAP services in this way, managers should reassure returning traumatized employees that the company wants to provide whatever help may be needed to assist in the employee's recovery. For example, if the traumatic experience was being fired, the EAP may help in a job search. If the problem is alcoholism or other substance abuse, the EAP may assist in finding a local group or residential program if needed. Managers may communicate the message that the company wants you to be healthy and that the company is proud of its employees who are courageous enough to want to be healthy and productive.

Explain to returning employees that there is no stigma attached to seeing an EAP counselor. Assure them that this will not cause a problem with the department or office either, since almost everyone is likely, at one time or another, to have situations come up where they need help in resolving some issue in their work environment.

In addition to TLEs, the reasons employees seek help from an EAP specialist in their companies are many and varied. Some may come for help in career counseling, job relocation, stress management, or conflict resolution. Many have financial questions about company benefits, retirement programs, union regulations, and payroll deductions. Others may face difficulty in areas of their home life and need help with preventive health care, diet, and nutrition, parenting, adoption, childcare, and deadbeat spouses. Still others file grievances in the workplace dealing with coworker bullies, control-freak bosses, sexual harassment, abusive managers, or alcohol-dependent or drug-using colleagues.

Human resources people recognize that employees often confront personal problems that can negatively impact their work performance. The aim of an EAP is to help troubled employees search for solutions to problems and return them to their best level of workplace performance.

A well-designed EAP is cost effective. It can increase productivity, make managing easier, reduce absenteeism, and lower attrition. Companies can't afford to lose good employees these days. The estimated cost to a company for each person replaced, according to social worker Mark Gorkin, is equal to at least one year's salary for that individual.

The Growth of EAPs

EAP programs have changed and grown since the first "Occupational Alcohol Program" of the 1940s. The range of services provided by today's EAP professionals has broadened to include marriage and family issues, stress-related problems, financial and legal difficulties, and psychological and workplace conflict. In fact, the website for the University of Texas Southwestern Medical Center's EAP program opens with this poster, indicating the incredible spread of issues dealt with by today's EAP professionals in large organizations and corporations.

EAP professional counselors in organizations today provide confidential assessment and short-term counseling to employees and their families to help them deal with any of these issues.

The number of government agencies and companies supporting EAP programs has also increased substantially. The business community has recognized that many everyday life stresses can negatively affect employee attendance and concentration, general workplace morale, and an employee's

Do any of these apply to you or you or your family?

Family Problems	Single Parenting	Dual Careers
Anxiety	Depression	Parent/Child/Conflict
Job Burnout	Divorce	Career Change
Financial Pressures	Physical Abuse	Life Transition
Communication	Alcohol or Drugs	Aging Problems
Unresolved Grief	Marital Problems	Sexual Problems
Personal Concerns	Stress	Eating Disorders
Problems of Adolescence	Relationship Issues	Legal Issues

ability to perform well on the job. Today, many companies have increased EAP services for their employees because they can measure the results in productivity and profits. For example, the American Mental Health Association estimates that 10–15 percent of employees have severe personal problems.

The EAP has over five thousand members in over thirty countries around the globe. It is the world's most relied upon source of information and support for and about employees. It offers training and other resources to fulfill its mission. It promotes the highest standards for professional programs and services. In the United States more than 97 percent of companies with more than five thousand employees have EAPs. A 2008 National Study of Employers following ten-year trends related to US workplace policies and benefits shows that the EAP industry continues to grow, with 65 percent of employers providing EAPs in 2008, up from 56 percent in 1998. The United States has the most saturated market for EAPs in the world. However, there is an ever-increasing appreciation of the value of employee assistance in other countries, and the number of EAPs worldwide is growing.

Some of the benefits of an EAP are seen in how a company's worker's compensation, drug, medical, and disability costs are reduced when employees use EAP services. Research has shown that since the 9/11 attacks, a third of businesses have increased their EAP services, which resulted in a large percentage of employees with improved attitudes. US Postal Service has reported almost two million dollars in savings after their employees began using EAP services.

As we have shown, traumatic events, even though they may happen outside the workplace, have a strong impact on the productive effectiveness of those traumatized by them. In these cases the goal of the EAP is to put the person in touch with the proper healthcare professional to brief the traumatized person as soon as possible and see that they receive further therapeutic care, as needed.

Typically, a traumatized person requires more than a debriefing. Some need weeks and months of therapy. As I have pointed out before, therapists can do only so much for a traumatized person, since they see the client only one hour at a time, usually once a week. If the trauma survivor has returned to the workplace, the person's manager and coworkers who see the survivors for eight hours every workday have many opportunities of supporting—or destabilizing—the work of the professional therapist.

It is surprising how many managers and other employees presume that the job of helping a person recover from a TLE belongs solely to the EAP professionals of an organization. A further false assumption that managers make is that when the TLE employee return to the job, "all that other emotional stuff" has been taken care of. The fact is it hasn't. The emotional stuff is still there, affecting not only the survivor but also the whole team.

A Case Study

I am continually amazed at how unsophisticated our organizations are in understanding and dealing with individuals who have experienced a TLE and are making a reentry to the workplace. My purpose is to provide a clear and accurate look at the behavior of managers and coworkers in dealing with traumatized employees in today's organizational settings.

The organization from which this case study is taken is one of the largest government agencies in Washington, DC. However, I find it is no different from any other organization where people are concerned with serving their constituents and customers.

Stanton Stone is a middle manager in the Division of Personnel. He is one of fifteen employees who manage a large segment of this agency. He has amassed a total of thirty-two years of government service, including service in the Air Force. In his late fifties, he is tall with grayish hair and can be described as Anglo. To his peers he is a walking encyclopedia of historical knowledge within the agency. He is respected by his colleagues and all those who have worked for him. He has received numerous awards. He enjoys the camaraderie of senior management officials in the agency, since he is frequently called upon to brief them in his areas of personnel expertise.

In all his years of work, except for an occasional cold, flu, or sinus condition, Stanton rarely complained of any serious physical ailments. However, two-and-a-half years ago, Stanton suffered a heart attack at his home in Vienna, Virginia. On a Saturday afternoon while gardening, he felt pains in his chest. Rushed to the hospital, he was scheduled for bypass surgery within a few days. Stanton was out of work for ten weeks following his surgery. His government health plan covered all his hospital, physician, and physical therapy expenses.

When he talked about his life before his trauma, he said that his work world had resolved around preparation for hearings on Capitol Hill and buyout legislation. His calendar was always filled with appointments and meetings. The trauma was an emotional shock, because for three months he played no part in the organization. His life was devoid of all the usual wonderful excitement and challenge.

Moreover, he said, he had always been an independent person, but after the trauma he had become physically and mentally dependent on others. His recuperation from surgery fell hard on him and his family. His two teenage children were afraid he might die. He kept trying to reassure them that everything was going to be all right. He said his wife had to make the biggest transition in learning to pay bills and maintaining the household, doing things he had done for twenty-five years. Stanton said, "Although I had little to do and few responsibilities, it was a very stressful time."

His convalescence took longer than expected because minor complications set in after the surgery. He experienced severe sporadic pain in his back and was diagnosed as having sleep apnea.

When I asked Stanton what his superiors had done for him during his recuperation period, I expected him to mention things like, "They saw that I got counseling, they came for personal visits, and they found ways of staying connected to me." But none of these gestures of human care had happened.

When he returned to work, he experienced a real dichotomy between the response of his colleagues and that of upper management. His colleagues, he said, were interested in what had happened to him; they were supportive and assured him they would be there for him if he needed anything.

In contrast, managers and senior staff who came by to say hello stayed in his cubicle "all of eight seconds." They were not unkind, he acknowledged, but neither did they show an interest in his condition or how he was faring as he reentered the work community. As Stanton explained, "They just left all that to me. Basically, over time, I found it very frustrating. They really had no interest in how I was doing. I was left alone to drift through the process of reentry and cope with it as best I could." He explained, "After years when you had been a focus of attention for all your colleagues, now you are not sure of yourself. You feel out of control." From his own experience he observed, "Physical recovery may take less time than emotional recovery, but emotional recovery is just as important even if it takes a longer time."

Because he had to drive a number of miles in rush hour traffic to the office each day, he became fatigued easily. Gradually, he negotiated with his supervisors to work three days at the office and two days at home mainly because of his continued back pain, fatigue, and long commute. He says this arrangement worked. With regard to productivity, management was willing to provide him with any computer technology he needed to do his job, but they offered him nothing emotionally.

Stanton and Ted

Prior to Stanton's heart bypass surgery he had supervised an employee named Ted, a professional personnel specialist who worked mostly in classification and compensation. At fifty years old, Ted stayed generally in good health. Soon after Stanton came to manage this division, Ted was scheduled for brain tumor surgery at Johns Hopkins University in Baltimore, Maryland. The surgery was classified as experimental, because it involved new procedures.

In learning of this new and untried surgery, Stanton found it very scary. A tumor had been found Ted's pituitary gland, and to remove it the surgeon would have to go into the center of the brain using a laser procedure, which was new at the time. The operation was reported a success. When Ted returned to work, there was no apparent disability or lack of ability to do his job, and he picked up rather quickly. But Stanton said he noticed that Ted wanted to continually talk about his brain tumor and surgery. He would volunteer this information to anyone who would listen. He might stop one of his colleagues and go into a long description of the specifics of his surgery, explaining certain details of his experience, for example, how he lost his sense of taste and smell or how he remembered smelling burning flesh during the operation. Naturally, some coworkers found this very unpleasant and felt embarrassed or annoyed. Some would avoid Ted. Stanton referred him to employee assistance program for counseling, which Ted appreciated.

After a while Ted had a relapse. He suffered a small stroke and lost his memory. When he returned to work again, he had only a short-attention span. Ted was aware of this, and when someone approached him about it, he became defensive. Again, Stanton referred him to EAP for personal therapy.

As his supervisor, Stanton stated, "Ted was able to do his work but I was not sure of my role as manager. I really didn't feel that I knew what I should be doing or not doing. I had no idea how to help him deal with the situation. I certainly felt that I wasn't really prepared. No one in the EAP ever came to me to tell me how I might be help in Ted's recovery or what I should tell Ted's coworkers about relating to him."

Stanton's Dilemma as a Manager

As organizations are continually challenged to deal with traumatized employees, managers feel they lack the necessary skills to understand what the traumatized person needs when they return to the workplace. As I talked with Stanton about his experience in relating to Ted, he said, "Knowing what I know now, both from my own experience and the experience with Ted and some other employees who have had traumatic experiences, I wish I had clear and specific information about how to relate to them before they had come back."

He said, "Next, I would like to be more sensitive to the returning employee. I would like to be able to explore with them how they were feeling as they returned to the workplace, what amount of work they felt capable of doing at the time, and what their concerns were in getting their jobs done. Ted never gave me the opportunity to talk in a private setting. I fault myself for not taking the initiative. I took the easy way out and let him volunteer information, instead of helping him talk about his feelings in a safe environment."

Stanton and I talked about what employees go through when they have TLEs, especially when they lose their jobs. We talked about what managers think and feel who have to deal with such people. Stanton had strong feelings on this subject. He believed, "Upper management gives only lip service and very sporadic communication about traumatized employees, leaving immediate supervisors, coworkers, and returning workers to fend for themselves."

Ted's Dilemma as an Employee

Executives and management in organizations tend to minimize the impact of a trauma on an employee. Coworkers are unsure of how to behave and often purposely avoid talking to the reentry employee, behaving as though their traumatic experience had never occurred. In most organizations, the current workplace atmosphere is not a healthy situation for the survivor, coworkers, or the manager of the group.

Stanton agreed. "Returning employees here," he said, "have not been dealt with in any sensitive manner. Little is done to let them express their concerns or feelings. It certainly is a bad situation that has an impact on productivity and people's motivation."

Now that Stanton had gone through a trauma himself, he felt he would be more sensitive to a reentry person's needs. If needed, he said he would search out a close friend of the traumatized employee to get information, or go to the employee assistance office and "ask them to tell me how I can help the person. I would find a way to be helpful."

During his interview with me, he would stop talking at times and just stare into space, perhaps recalling his first days back on the job. He repeatedly said that no senior managers reached out to help him. "People were superficially reassuring, but felt no depth to their feelings." Then, he said, "I would like to know how to make it easier for the reentry person."

The Benefits of Knowledge

To be helpful and not harmful to the emotional recovery process, managers and coworkers will need to learn new skills with a focus on knowing how to communicate well, engage in interpersonal dialogue, and refer employees to appropriate human resources and healthcare services. The Dialogue Circle format, which I discuss in detail in Part II of this book, provides a simple and easy way to gain much of this knowledge.

Learning these skills is also good business. Caring communication between a manager and an employee upon their reentry after a trauma can derail a possible grievance or Equal Employment Opportunity (EEO) complaint. For example, the manager who takes the time to openly approach and talk to a returning TLE employee is not only assisting the employee's return but reestablishing the manager's credibility with the employee as a trusting and compassionate person. A manager who continues to create such a caring atmosphere over the long term can diffuse the anger of reentry employees and help them reappraise a difficult situation more positively.

Unfortunately, today's managers are not given policy guidelines or an organizational format dealing with employees who are returning to the workplace after experiencing a trauma. Survivors who return need a consciously designed emotional framework that will facilitate and support their reentry. Hopefully, organizations will begin to recognize this need as an opportunity and will begin to support an intervention designed to create an ambiance that reaches out to returning TLE employees without emotionally harming them.

Long working hours and demanding deadlines create an environment for competitiveness in performance. Without sensitivity toward returning traumatized employees, performance problems can arise or increase, creating another layer of communication hurdles for a manager. The human resources department and the organization can work together, through appropriate education, to reach out to these employees who must find their way through a necessary process of healing and emotional recovery.

The Dialogue Circle, focused on understanding the emotional recovery of trauma for managers and employees, provides a simple, not-very-time-consuming way to educate people in an office about what to expect from employees returning to the workplace after a TLE. The Dialogue Circle does not replace employees' likely need for private counseling or group therapy. Nor does it teach the manager how to deal with employees' emotional problems the way a therapist would. It does, however, educate managers about three critical areas in the reentry process: the successive stages most trauma survivors go through in their emotional recovery, how these survivors are likely to behave when they first return to work, and the workplace context of safety and support survivors will need to make the reentry smoothly and effectively.

The Dialogue Circle for managers and coworkers brings them new knowledge that can generate powerful, though hard-to-quantify, benefits. With such education and coaching, managers and coworkers can learn to feel more confident in how they respond to a returning TLE employee. When trauma survivors return to a workplace that provides a safe haven for them, a willing ear to listen to their trauma experience, and a helping hand to reestablish connections to the workplace family, they are more likely to recover more quickly and become once again fully productive members of the workplace team.

Trauma and its effects cover every facet of our lives from childhood to adulthood, from birth to death. Understanding it will help many on the road to recovery from a traumatic event.

The next phase addresses how managers and coworkers can learn to intervene helpfully with a TLE employee. They do this by defining effective techniques for reintegrating trauma survivors. For that we need to understand the dynamics of the Dialogue Circle.

PART II

TAKING PRACTICAL STEPS

CHAPTER EIGHT

~

What Is a Dialogue Circle?

An Adult Learning Format

A Dialogue Circle is an adult learning format with a wide range of applications. In general, it is designed to help participants who lack information in a certain area. It is especially useful in helping a small group of people going through a similar life transition or in coping with an important situation in which they are all invested. For this reason, Dialogue Circles may be used in many different areas of life and to cope with many different issues, not merely dealing with TLEs.

For example, one Dialogue Circle might involve a group of parents all struggling to cope with their hyperactive children. Another might bring together a group of citizens to grasp the implications of an amendment on the voting ballot. A professor or student might use a Dialogue Circle with a group interested in appreciating poetry or learning a foreign language. A church community may want to create a group of people trying to apply scriptural writings to their lives. Concerned citizens could gather a group of concerned farmers exploring the pros and cons of genetically altered crops. The workplace may want to learn ways to resist sexual harassment in the office. For us, the Dialogue Circle topic is how to deal with employees returning to the workplace after a TLE.

The Dialogue Circle may also be used as a tool for enrichment and as a tool to affect change, as with the Dialogue Circle on understanding the emotional recovery of trauma.

I selected the Dialogue Circle method of intervention for dealing with trauma in the workplace because it allows managers and employees to come together to share their views and focus on this specific topic. Dialogue Circles promote both group interaction and collective sharing of ideas and information among participants. In a Dialogue Circle, all individual views are considered, and participants have an opportunity to listen, converse, and disagree.

A Dialogue Circle is a democratic form of group learning in which five to fifteen people with a common interest gather to investigate a particular topic. Some topics require few sessions; others require more. The Dialogue Circle on workplace trauma needs three sessions.

Working together, circle participants learn from each other, from prepared materials and from outside sources. One handout page was all we needed for each session of the Dialogue Circle on workplace trauma. It contained a few definitions and some questions for discussion. No instructor teaches or controls the circle. Led by a facilitator trained in group dynamics and the Dialogue Circle concept, the participants learn from each other's knowledge and experience.

The Dialogue Circle format calls for a facilitator who can give the group members focus, foster discussion, and encourage everyone's ownership of the topic. The facilitator does not teach and is not required to be an expert in the subject under discussion, but must be familiar enough with the topic to raise questions for the group. The facilitator helps create and maintain a collaborative learning atmosphere where each participant feels free to express ideas, relate personal experiences, and discuss points of view on the subject. A successful facilitator will be a good listener, who quickly gets to know the members, gains their confidence, and encourages their participation. This form of learning had some interesting beginnings.

Historical Background of Dialogue Circles

Dialogue Circles as a distinct form of education emerged in the United Stated during the latter half of the nineteenth century as one element of the Chautauqua Movement, a name derived from Lake Chautauqua, a famous campsite where Sunday School meetings were held. Bishop John H. Vincent created Dialogue Circle groups from the individuals who attended the Chautauqua Literary and Scientific Circle (CISC). Here, people met in small group to study subjects such as history, art, languages, and literature. Many were adults who had never gone to college but who wanted to continue their education. Others among them who had undergraduate degrees wanted to expand their knowledge. CISC members were perhaps first among Americans to practice "lifelong learning." The organization developed printed study circles materials for these courses.

In the early days, bible study for adults became another favorite Dialogue Circle topic, since scriptural classes were then available only in seminaries and ministerial colleges. Soon, social and political topics were added to the Dialogue Circle curriculum.

Without a formal "teacher" to lead them, participants in these circles developed a fresh collaborative and interactive approach to adult learning and education, different from the traditional classroom format. The Dialogue Circle's interactive model places importance on learning in a social context, not in isolation. Among adults, as experts have discovered, learning is best accomplished by doing and participating, and as a result producing participants who are changed and more experienced.

During the last quarter of the nineteenth century, Dialogue Circle groups might meet in a church basement, in a back room at a restaurant, in someone's home or anywhere participants could arrange half a dozen chairs in a circle. The Dialogue Circle proved itself as an effective learning tool because, unlike a classroom or lecture format, participants were actively involved in the learning process. They became involved because the subject matter impacted their lives and welfare. Typically, during these sessions bonds of mutual concern began to form between participants, and individuals seemed more personally interested in each other than before. I might mention that I have noticed these positive effects in all of the Dialogue Circles on trauma and emotional recovery that I have facilitated.

As the Dialogue Circle in its early days expanded into political topics and public affairs issues, it became a way to educate Americans about political life, democratic methods, community problems, and social concerns. After reading a page or two of information about the topic under discussion, Dialogue Circle participants could voice their opinions, share their experiences, present their resources, ask questions, identify problems, and build consensus toward solutions. Most importantly, they learned from one another, they clarified their views, let go of unwarranted assumptions, and discovered they each had something to contribute.

By 1878, fifteen thousand home Dialogue Circles were meeting regularly across America using the Chautauqua approach as their form of education and discussion.

At that time in the United States, there was a great desire for learning among the adult industrialized urban population, many of whom could not afford to leave their jobs to attend college. Organizers of adult civic educational programs offered one solution. They were promoting educational formats involving large public lecture halls and school auditoriums, including the Lyceum Movement, the University Extension Movement, and the Studebaker Public Forum Movement. Such organizers were less interested in small group learning formats where people came together to discuss issues and exchange ideas. Nevertheless, in response to this widespread need and desire for college credits, CISC developed a four-year correspondence study based on Home Dialogue Circles.

The Dialogue Circle Moves to Sweden

Oscar Olson of the Swedish temperance movement visited the United States in 1889 and took the Dialogue Circle idea back to Sweden. Olson became known at the "father of the Dialogue Circle" there, after these circles proved to be an effective mechanism for recruiting and educating members of the temperance movement.

During the nineteenth century, Sweden was a bleak nation; its social discontent created a demand for social change. Popular movements began to emerge, including the temperance movement, the free-church movement, and the blue collar industrial unions. These movements gave the people a framework and a taste for self-governments as they fought for basic rights within their society. The leaders of these movements realized that the education of their undereducated members would help bring about a major change in Swedish society. Here's where the Dialogue Circle came in. Not only did it serve as a vehicle for many popular movements to advance their causes and create opportunities for the education of their people, but more importantly it also brought all types of people together. Dialogue Circles were originally called Study Circles and a first book was published on Study Circles in 1987, titled *Study Circles: Coming Together for Personal Growth and Social Change*, by Leonard P. Oliver. It stated that "following World War II the Study Circle was the most important form of adult civic education in Sweden."[1]

After the war, Sweden's Dialogue Circle activities became even more extensive, involving members of political and religious parties and intramural departments. According to Oliver, "The Swedish government recognized and formalized the practice and organizational structure of Dialogue Circles in 1947 by introducing government grants to subsidize the cost of leader salaries and materials."[2] With the approval of these grants, according to Oliver, came a definition of Dialogue Circles as "an informal group which meets for the common pursuit of well-planned studies of a subject or problem area which has previous been decided upon."

In Sweden the use of Dialogue Circles was focused on a simple goal, to promote empowered citizens. For the Swedes, a citizen is empowered by taking part in dialogues about complex issues, where each citizen has a voice and is heard. In Sweden, Dialogue Circles became a way of life, where many adults attended sessions in homes, churches, and meeting halls.

Dialogue Circles in the United States since 1970

Almost a century after the Dialogue Circle was born—and almost disappeared in the United States—it was rediscovered. N. D. Kurland, then Executive Director of Adult Learning Services of the New York State Education Department, traveled in Sweden and Denmark to study the use of Dialogue Circles there. He described his findings in his article "The Scandinavian Study Circle: An Idea for the United States." Based upon his research and with support from the Rockefeller Brothers Fund and the New York State Education Department, he sought to revive the Dialogue Circle concept in the United States. His plan took root in New York where the New York State Dialogue Circle Consortium was established consisting of eight public and private institutions of high education. In 1980, the consortium ran four hundred Dialogue Circle programs across the state in various institutions.

Although this approach has not been followed by other states, the Dialogue Circle movement on its own momentum has grown extensively in recent years. For example, the National Issues Forums supported by the Kettering Institute, has during the 1980s and 1990s sponsored up to five thousand Dialogue Circles each year throughout the United States under the auspices of its institution's educational nonprofit branch.

Enter the Dialogue Circle Organization Today

Currently, the Study Circle Resource Center is located in Pomfret, Connecticut, where it was originally founded by Paul J. Aicher. It became a clearinghouse for information about Dialogue Circle activities all over the country providing training material to groups interested in conducting programs.

The Study Circle Resource Center, which was created in 1989, was renamed and is now called Everyday Democracy. It has become a national organization that helps local communities develop their own ability to self-organize large-scale and diverse participation in dialogue structured to support and strengthen measurable community change. They work with neighborhoods, cities and towns, regions and states, paying particular attention to the racial and ethnic dimensions of community problems, such as poverty reduction, education reform, and building strong neighborhoods. Their ultimate aim is to help create communities that value everyone's voice and work for everyone, and to help create a strong national democracy that upholds these principles. Dialogue Circles are at the heart of their process for public dialogue and community change.

Dialogue Circles Used in Organizations

Although most Dialogue Circles are community based, I have found a few reported examples of Dialogue Circles that are corporate based, which shows that the Dialogue Circles are slowly making their way into the organizational life of the United States.

Since the latter part of the 1980s, Dialogue Circles have been used by organizations such as the International Union of Bricklayers and Allied Craftsman Organization. This is a one hundred thousand–member craft union, who adopted Dialogue Circles for its member education. They trained Dialogue Circle facilitators, published materials and formed twenty-seven Dialogue Circles. With their success they published a newsletter with strong support from union membership, trained two hundred local leaders, and developed a Dialogue Circle curriculum that covers topics such as union organizing and health care issues.

At around the same time, DeRidder-Thurtson, Inc., a manufacturing corporation in Rochester, New York, had concerns with employee motivation and wanted to raise the level of productivity. Among the various techniques available, the staff chose to introduce Dialogue Circles for employees because the concept covered their educational and social needs as well as the employer's needs. The goal was "getting people to work together." Dialogue Circles proved to be very effective in getting people at all levels to talk together, which led to more cooperative efforts at work.

My own experience using Dialogue Circles in the federal government proved very successful in educating managers and coworkers about the issues faced by employee returning to work after having a TLE. After attending the three sessions of this Dialogue Circle, managers reported feeling more confident in approaching such returning employee, having concrete examples of what to do and what not to do, and feeling better equipped than before for interacting with employees returning to work after a TLE. Coworkers learned that each person handles trauma in their own way, how one person's trauma can change the atmosphere and attitudes of the team, and how important it is for the entire team to know how to handle the situation.

Dialogue Circles and Group Participation

It is difficult to predict which participants will profit most from a Dialogue Circle. Sometimes, the most silent or least obvious contributors may be the ones who develop the most learning and skills, while the most vocal or active participants may be the ones who, personally, gain the least, even if they seem to have contributed the most.

False assumptions can also inhibit any form of group communication. We can falsely assume we know what others mean when they speak, and others may falsely assume they know what we mean when we speak. In any group, it is likely that each person hears the speaker's message differently and interprets that same message in a different way. After all, each person comes into a group with a personal agenda and for personal reasons. Usually, they are asking themselves, "What do I want to get from this group?" The same is true in a Dialogue Circle, which is why the facilitator's role is so important.

At times individuals may gather in a Dialogue Circle group to discuss very sensitive issues such as race relations and spousal abuse. Peoples' strong feelings on such volatile issues may give rise to unexpected outbursts of emotion. As a rule emotional outbursts should be handled on a one-on-one basis.

Individual feelings and opinions are often expressed during the Dialogue Circle. Therefore, if an outburst occurs, the facilitator ensures that each person in the Dialogue Circle is given a chance to share his point of view, including the person who may have caused the disruption. After all the participants have had an opportunity to talk about what occurred, the Dialogue Circle continues.

By ensuring that everyone's views are considered during the discussion, it expands everyone's horizons. In this way, the Dialogue Circle's informal process represents an advance in adult pedagogy because it provides an opportunity for an expression of genuine democracy in local problem solving of community and public issues. The solutions are securely built on the rich experience and combined knowledge of the group. The Dialogue Circle process provides the essential link between learning and life and, in the workplace, between learning and working together.

The Dialogue Circle shows people that they can have a voice in their civic or corporate community and the policies that are being made. The

Dialogue Circle approach is unique in that it encourages people to formulate their own ideas and share them with others, something seldom done in large meeting halls, public hearing, training sessions, or lectures. It is a powerful vehicle for involving people at a fundamental level in the life of their community or organization. It encourages members to become their own experts and to take responsibility for making needed changes.

Since the first publication of my book, I have given numerous Dialogue Circles throughout the states. I found them to be very helpful to the participants and to myself as facilitator and observer.

I recently gave two Dialogue Circles. The first one was to the Jungian Society in Washington, DC. This group was an eclectic group where each person had survived a unique type of trauma and wanted to share it with the group. The dialogue was interesting and participants allowed all the members to share and learn from each other. The second Dialogue Circle was presented at St. Peter's Episcopal Church in Lewes, Delaware. Here I gave a combination lecture and presentation where I broke up the groups into four Dialogue Circles after my presentation. I walked around and observed individuals interacting with each other and noticed some people listening and others sharing their trauma stories. This reinforced the cognitive learning that occurs during this process.

Driven by Need

Since Dialogue Circles are driven primarily by participants' needs, it is appropriate that the content or subject matter should create the need and motivation for the Dialogue Circle. However, in a Dialogue Circle the *process is just as important* as the *topic*. Individuals meet and share their experiences about the topic, but the actual learning in a Dialogue Circle occurs collectively when participants hear and relate their personal experience to that of the group.

In each of the Dialogue Circle sessions on workplace trauma that I led, managers and employees practiced active listening skills and received feedback from participants when retelling their trauma stories. One manager shared the story of her trauma when her fiancée was diagnosed with cancer. At the time, she was on an upward career path but felt she had to refocus her energies to take care of him. She found her anxiety level was escalating and noticed that she was exhibiting behaviors that she did not view as normal. Because of her fiancée's serious illness she too was traumatized and she constantly talked about what she was experiencing. She stated that talking about it was how she "coped." Participants asked her questions and wanted to learn from her experience. People who had family members with cancer or other terminal illnesses learned from her ways of coping with it. Participants who did not have such a family member became more sensitive and compassionate toward those who did.

The Dialogue Circle process is not only self-directed and interactive; it is also dynamic and practical. After each Dialogue Circle session, participants begin immediately using what they have learned.

One manager, commenting on the timeliness of the Trauma Dialogue Circle for her, stated that within a week of the first session two employees under her care experienced deaths in their family. After listening to the participants exchange ideas in the first Dialogue Circle session, she was able to offer a better level of comfort to these employees upon their return to work. This was something she did not know how to do prior to the Dialogue Circle.

Experienced-Based Learning

Theorists in adult education usually define mature learning as the *transformation of experience into knowledge, skills, and attitudes.* For adults, all learning has an experiential basis. Adults learn best by doing and participating in small groups, thus they are mutually recreating each other so that each participant is changed and grows wiser. Participants seek to assimilate information in a way that influences their circumstances.

Participants stated that "hearing other people tell their stories," "how they handled their trauma," and "what worked and what did not work" was important for them to hear. Another participant said, "All of the sessions were helpful, especially the last two, when several people opened up and shared their experiences."

People have an innate desire to learn. Observing the growth of participants' knowledge and their improving ability to understand and interact with the people around them during a Dialogue Circle session is in itself sufficient payback for their effort. Learning is its own reward.

An interactive learning experience allows for a variety of responses. Growth in knowledge can occur in many different ways, with outcomes personalized to each participant. In a Dialogue Circle, people learn in a participatory environment, continually reflecting on and integrating new information. Participants are enabled to put their lives into perspective and to see their own viewpoints in wider social context. Adult education is meant to be a living, active process that relates knowledge to action and change, to growth and creativity, to social sensitivity and collective development. The Dialogue Circle process is designed to produce all of these.

The Dialogue Circle:
An Educational Format for the Organization

Traditionally, in the workplace the three most common education formats are the lecture, the seminar, and the workshop.

The *lecture* is best for communicating and clarifying information, procedures, policies, regulations, and the like. It is also used by executives to stir and motivate employees.

The *seminar* format is most often used by corporate leadership to explore and formulate new ideas, policies, and procedures. It allows participants to debate and discuss them before implementing them.

The *workshop* is used primarily for training people in various skills; it is a very practical educational model with developing a very specific performance skill in the learners as its main purpose. It is usually run by trainers who are experts in that skill.

What has been missing in the workplace is *an educational process for dealing with topics that need to be learned attitudinally*, that is, topics that are aimed at transforming not only knowledge and behavior but also attitudes and emotions. In dealing with the reentry of a traumatized employee, it is not enough to present the kinds of knowledge and information given in a lecture, nor is it enough to include a set of behavioral skills that one might learn in a workshop. The "missing" educational format needs also to provide ways to educate attitudes and emotions as well. The Dialogue Circle provides this missing dimension of the traditional learning process in the workplace.

The personal sharing in the Dialogue Circle by participants who had experienced a traumatic life event or had managed a returning TLE employee provided the context for the needed attitudinal and emotional learning to take place in a practical and realistic way. For example, consider Gwen's story. If she was absent from your office and came back to work a week after her TLE, would you know how to deal with her—what to say and what not to way, what to do and what not to do—if you were her manager or one of her coworkers? Here's her story.

Gwen, who worked as one of a large group of claims processors for a major health insurance company, went home as usual after work last Tuesday. She got off her bus and stopped at the local market for a few things she needed for dinner that evening. When she opened the door of the apartment, some things just didn't look right but it wasn't enough to bother her. Her eight-year-old daughter was watching television.

"Daddy left an envelope for you on the kitchen table," the girl said.

Gwen walked into the kitchen, unsealed the envelope, read the note, and stood there in shock. In the note, George, her husband of ten years, announced that he had taken his things and had left to start a new life. "I'm not ever coming back," was the last line of the note.

As she walked around in a daze, Gwen realized the house had looked unusual because George had removed various things, including the stereo and the CD collection that went with it, all his sports equipment, his clothing, and his laptop computer. When she saw the empty garage, she realized George had also taken the family car. The next morning Gwen would discover he had also wiped clean both their checking account and their savings account.

"Did daddy say where he was going?" Gwen cautiously asked her daughter.

"I didn't see him at all." She replied. "He must have left before I got home."

"How did you know about the note he left for me?" she asked

"I saw it when I was getting milk and cookies," said her daughter.

Gwen realized her daughter was totally unaware that her father had abandoned both of them.

Next morning, Gwen telephoned her manager at work and said she would be taking a few days of personal leave.

"Sure, Gwen," the manager said. "We'll cover for you. But are you all right? I hope nothing is wrong with you or your family?"

"It's nothing. I just need a few days to straighten out some things here," she answered.

Gwen wasn't about to tell him that her husband had just left them without any warning or money, and that he had probably run off with his pretty secretary, a supposition that later turned out to be true. It was painfully embarrassing to have to shift in a moment from being a contented wife and mother to being someone your husband would drop, disown, steal from, and replace with a younger more attractive model. "I'm a failure as a wife," she said to herself.

Eventually, people at work will have to learn about this, she thought, but not yet. "How can I ever face the people I work with?" she said aloud, as she pictured people looking from their desks at her the day she walked into work for the first time. She felt ashamed just thinking about it.

Undoubtedly, her manager, when he discovers Gwen's situation and predicament, will refer her to human resources for counseling and legal assistance. But, how should her manager and coworkers treat her? As if all her troubles were none of their business? As if nothing bad had ever happened? As if everything was back to normal now? Or should they pity her behind her back?

Such treatment could easily reinforce her shame and embarrassment, convince her that she had been a bad wife and mother, and prove that she was not someone worth showing compassion toward. None of this would help Gwen's recovery, rebuild her spirit of work, and get her back feeling a part of the team.

Moreover, there is no simple formula on what to say or do in dealing in a caring manner with a returning employee like Gwen. Each trauma survivor is a unique personality with different needs and expectations. For Gwen, even though in the long—and short—run resolving her financial situation would be more crucial, her main concern was her shame and embarrassment returning to the workplace.

Only in hearing a number of trauma stories and talking them over, as would happen in a Dialogue Circle, would the participants come to develop a sense of or attitude toward the emotional recovery process for survivors like Gwen.

If the Dialogue Circle process was working well, after hearing her story, participants would be asking themselves, "How can I help *put out a welcome mat* for Gwen? How can I *lend a listening ear* to let her tell her story to me if she wants to? How can I *offer a helping hand* to help her reconnect so that she really feels a valuable part of our team again?" And each one would be sharing thoughts and ideas with the other participants.

The Dialogue Circle's Democratic Spirit

Another educational dynamic characteristic of the Dialogue Circle process is its "democratic" spirit. When properly conducted, a Dialogue Circle makes every participant equal and values everyone's contribution. This democratic spirit in the traumatic event Dialogue Circle allows managers and employees to share their experiences and discuss the topic as equals. A rather revolutionary event in corporate life!

Whereas the task of helping the successful reentry of a TLE employee would normally fall to a counselor or therapist, the Dialogue Circle format allows workplace participants, not to assume the role of the therapist, but to learn to support and promote the therapeutic work in ways appropriate to managers and coworkers.

An adequate understanding of this "work of support" that can be provided by managers and coworkers could not have happened through a traditional lecture or workshop, but only in a holistic learning format where personal experience and empathy along with the expression of attitudes, emotions, and values are included. The Dialogue Circle format puts these experiential and emotional factors at the center of its learning process.

The Dialogue Circle as an educational format can also prove useful with a topic around which organizational policies and procedures have *not yet* been formulated and institutionalized. Treatment of the returning TLE employee by managers and coworkers is one such focus. Because such treatment requires a major involvement with empathy, attitudes, and emotional sensitivity, it is not an appropriate topic for legislation by executives or presentation in a seminar. The Dialogue Circle format invites participants to share their personal views around such topics, and it views this personal experience as important data in helping shape procedures and policies. In summary, the Dialogue Circle process, as an adult learning format, can fill a missing dimension among the educational tools currently used in the organizational workplace.

The Dialogue Circle: A Psychological Process

Some may object to the claim that the Dialogue Circle is an education process, not primarily a psychological one. They may assert that the participants use the sessions as a psychological process, no matter what anyone may claim. "What you're promoting with a Dialogue Circle is nothing more than group therapy."

The Dialogue Circle is not a group therapy session. Although the two processes have some elements in common—both call for trust, group cohesion, and a willingness to share personal experiences—there are many elements that differentiate them. Each Dialogue Circle has its own specific topic, for example, "the returning TLE employee," while the topic of group therapy is always the same—*the psychological health of the individual group members*. In a Dialogue Circle, specific conceptual material is discussed, and the facilitator has a list of questions about the topic that help define the sequence of the process. Thus, each Dialogue Circle on the returning TLE will follow the same sequence, and in the end each Dialogue Circle group will have covered the same material. None of these elements is true of therapy groups.

Some have claimed that Dialogue Circles are merely another name for "rap groups." Although it is not a therapeutic intervention, the Dialogue Circle has elements similar to the rap group process, which is primarily therapeutic. Rap groups were introduced in 1970 by psychiatrists Jay Lifton and Chaim Shatan. They invited Vietnam veterans to retell their stories of war trauma to each other. Veterans who were "hurting" felt comfortable in this setting as it provided a safe context in which to reconstruct their trauma story outside of a traditional psychiatric setting. It was here in these rap groups that psychological trauma was first identified by the psychiatric professionals as a "real diagnosis." And eventually PTSD was recognized formally in its diagnostic manuals by the American Psychiatric Association.

The big distinction between the rap group and a Dialogue Circle is that the group members in a rap group are trying to heal themselves. In contrast, the people in a TLE Dialogue Circle are not trying to heal themselves but rather to understand the emotional process of recovery going on in their fellow employees returning to the workplace after a TLE.

It might be clarifying to make a few additional distinctions. First, although the Dialogue Circle *topic* might be concerned with a psychological process, for example, the psychological recovery of the TLE employee, such a topic may still be treated educationally—as having concepts and procedures to be identified, defined, and understood (i.e., learned). Thus, participants learned the concept of the "putting out a welcome mat" and the procedures for evoking "lending a listening ear."

Second, since the Dialogue Circle process involves the physical, mental, emotional, and social dimensions of all participants, it is not surprising that, during a Dialogue Circle, participants notice emotional and attitudinal changes happening in themselves as well as conceptual and behavioral ones. Good education always changes the whole person, not just the intellect. Moreover, workplace participants are more likely to notice the psychological dynamics happening in a Dialogue Circle, since in most other forms of workplace education such as lectures, seminars, and training workshops, psychological dynamics play a much less significant part.

Finally, it is not surprising that Dialogue Circle participants are very aware of the interplay of emotions and attitudes that happen among participants during the sessions. A Dialogue Circle wants to get participants emotionally involved. It is precisely because the participants are so involved that the Dialogue Circle process is as effective as an educational format. It allows people who have strong feeling about a certain topic to meet together in a structured learning process that encourages everyone to share their own personal experiences, not merely "thoughts," about the topic. The Dialogue Circle format ensures that this is done in ways that end up, not in debate and competition, but learning from each other.

Cognitive Learning

The Dialogue Circle's cognitive component helps the participants learn new responses from each other. They are able to develop and apply new behaviors related to what they learn. In a Dialogue Circle I conducted, one participant stated that it was important for the managers to show "empathy" toward the returning TLE employee. Participants then engaged in an intellectual discussion about the meaning of "empathy" and addressed their questions to each other on how a person shows empathy. This issue created an ongoing dialogue throughout the three Dialogue Circle sessions.

Another subject that provoked cognitive discussion among the managers was "productivity versus compassion." Some managers are concerned with recent downsizing within their organizations and loss of resources. Conflict and ambivalence surfaced among them when they started to differentiate between being concerned with "the bottom line" and showing "compassion" to the returning TLE employee.

The handouts provided by the researcher prior to each Dialogue Circle session also served as a cognitive learning resource to the participants. Both managers and employees referred to the helpfulness of these handouts that guided them through each session.

The Dialogue Circle educational model presented the participants with an opportunity to think, feel, and act differently about a new topic.

Affective Learning

In a Dialogue Circle, participants get in touch with their attitudes, feelings, and preferences regarding returning TLE employees. This occurs through the dialogue, sharing, interaction, and networking that is typically created among the participants. The Dialogue Circle facilitator allows the dialogue to emerge by letting participants ask each other questions and inquiring about the extent of their own traumas.

In one session I recall, when managers were discussing performance and behavioral problems of TLE employees, they felt that these problems could become serious if the persons were not supported in the workplace. After a session, it is not unusual that a few in the group remain in the room to keep talking about how to handle a returning TLE employee.

One manager, who had himself returned to work after surviving a traumatic event, expressed the importance of being hugged by a few people on his return and being made to feel welcomed back. He specifically mentioned the words "dialogue, sharing feelings, and physical association." He stated that all of these expressions of care meant a lot to him and he felt it would mean a lot to another person in the same situation.

Affective learning is accomplished in the Dialogue Circle sessions through interactions and discussions that allow managers and employees to become aware of each other's perceptions and feelings.

Now, the question is: How do we set up on-site Dialogue Circles for managers and coworkers to help them understand TLEs and understand the emotional recovery process of employees returning to the workplace after having a TLE?

Note

1. Leonard P. Oliver, *Study Circles: Coming Together for Personal Growth and Social Change* (Washington, DC: Seven Locks Press, 1987), 5.

2. Ibid.

CHAPTER NINE

~

How to Set Up a Dialogue Circle

Introduction

This chapter offers suggestions for selecting participants, procedures for conducting the Dialogue Circle, and the roles of participants and facilitator.

As I indicated earlier, Dr. Judith Lewis Herman in her book, *Trauma and Recovery* with a new epilogue in 2015, described three stages that are required for the successful recovery and reentry of the traumatized person into normal life. A major part of normal life is lived out in the workplace. Accordingly, these three stages were selected as the underlying themes in Dialogue Circle sessions.

Session 1. Putting out a welcome mat for the returning traumatized employee.

Session 2. Lending a listening ear for the person to tell their trauma experience.

Session 3. Offering a helping hand to reconnecting the returning employee to the work community.

The first session in the Dialogue Circle focuses on what putting out a welcome mat may mean to the survivor and how management can establish a safe haven for the returning TLE employee. A safe haven is a place where someone can go for comfort in trying to deal with their emotional pain. The welcome mat concept extends to a person's home and work environment and, in its broadest meaning, includes a safe living situation, financial security, mobility, and plan for self-protection. It may also include concern for the survivor's body and related basic health needs, sleep, eating, and exercise. Providing a safe place usually also encompasses a social support system that needs to be established for the survivors, specifically, people who will not tease, taunt, threaten, shame, or pressure them or pry into painful emotions and memories.

Putting out a welcome mat is important because, when a trauma occurs, survivors are likely to feel powerless and robbed of control over themselves. They may feel unsafe in relation to other people, especially if they are returning to work after a long absence. "Is my job still mine?" "Has someone else been doing it better in my absence?" "Will my coworkers welcome me back?" "Will they still like me?" These and many other questions go through their minds. Because of the time taken away from work by their traumatic experience, such returning employees may not know if and when they will get paid and if they can have additional time off if they need it. For them, these are issues of safety and security.

Consider the case of Gwen being abandoned by her husband, the story I told in the previous chapter. If she worked in your office, how would you begin to create a safe haven for her? How would you go about finding out what was worrying her, what questions she was asking herself about the people in her office, and how they would treat her on her return?

The second session discusses the usefulness of having returning employees reveal their trauma story to people in the workplace, including the pain they felt associated with the experience. And so it is important that fellow employees lend a listening ear to the returning person. Research has shown that storytelling is particularly important to trauma survivors when they return to work. But only when and if they are ready and willing to share their experience. Reconstructing the traumatic experience with colleagues is likely to be beneficial in the emotional recovery process, if it is done with care and concern. The discussion that happens in the second Dialogue Circle session focuses on whether, how, and when the trauma story can be reconstructed by the traumatized employees upon returning to the workplace, and how managers and coworkers might best help allow it to happen.

Could you guess a few reasons why Gwen would not want to elaborate on her story to her colleagues when she returned to work? Do you think Gwen would be ready to relate her whole story to you her first day back to work?

The theme of the Dialogue Circle's third session is all about reconnecting the reentry employee to the work community. This theme is important because returning TLE employees may need to reclaim their "lost world," reestablish relationships with managers and coworkers, and build a new workplace life. Here's where fellow employees can offer a helping hand to the returning person. The manager also plays a key role. In this session, the discussion usually revolves around the manager's role and how the manager can assist returning employees reconnect with their coworkers, a bond that survivors often feel they may have lost because of the trauma.

Gwen sees herself now as a very different person from the one she was who left work so happily last Tuesday. If you were her manager or a fellow employee reconnecting with her, should you try to reconnect with the old Gwen or the "different" Gwen?

Selecting Participants

Participants in any TLE Dialogue Circle should include both managers and employees. The managers observe the employees in this sharing dialogue, and employees observe the managers. If every participant hasn't had a personal TLE, they all know of others who have. If they personally don't know what it is like to reenter the workplace after having experienced a trauma, they have probably heard comments from those who have been through the process. When there is a mix of employees and managers, all gain awareness from each other on how to address the TLE employee reentering the workplace.

I suggest that the organization preparing to conduct this Dialogue Circle canvass for volunteers to participate. A Dialogue's Circle success depends on participants who are very interested and invested in the topic and *want* to participate.

I also suggest an invitation along with a confidential agreement be given to each participant before the first session (see samples at the end of this chapter). The invitation confirms the participant's role in the Dialogue Circle, and its confidential agreement protects any participant disclosing to others information of a personal nature heard during the Dialogue Circle sessions.

Remind participants of the time and place of each session with a telephone call or an email message.

A good mix of volunteers for a Dialogue Circle on returning traumatized employees would include people from the four following groups:

1. Managers who have supervised a returning TLE employee.
2. Managers who have not supervised a returning TLE employee.
3. Managers who have or have not had a personal TLE.
4. Employees who have experienced a TLE.

In recruiting participants for the Dialogue Circle, in addition to a mix of labor and management, a mix of personalities and roles is preferred. For example, if all participants in one group are accountants the session may not result in a conversation with diverse opinions because of the composition of the group. On the other hand, I have never facilitated a group that did not result in a rich conversation, no matter what the mix of participants.

A few—very few, in my experience—participants may refuse to become involved in the Dialogue Circle process. Some may be reticent to dialogue or share their thoughts with a group. For some of these, all they need is a word of encouragement from the facilitator and to be directly invited to participate. If a simple direct invitation doesn't work. I have found that if I make the effort to speak afterward with such a person in private, I can usually encourage them to be more forthcoming in the next session.

In your organization, it may be a human resources person who does the interviews, schedules the sessions, and acts as facilitator. Or it may be someone else. Interviews are not strictly necessary, as long as the participants are interested and have an investment in the topic.

Interviews

When I first began facilitating this TLE Dialogue Circle in my department in the federal government, I found it very useful to conduct individual Pre–Dialogue Circle interviews privately with members of each group, for several reasons. I used these interviews to provide participants with an overview of the scope and purpose of the Dialogue Circle, and to introduce the three Dialogue Circle themes, obtain some background information about them to familiarize myself with them, and learn about their own trauma stories.

In a few cases, for example, with people who were too close to their trauma and some who were still in shock, I discouraged them from attending. For example, I would discourage someone like Gwen from attending during the first few weeks after her return to work, since her traumatic experience may be still too raw and painful for her to benefit from the dialogue. But I would encourage her manager and coworkers to attend. Actually, I would wish they had participated in a TLE Dialogue Circle *before* Gwen had her TLE.

During these interviews I encourage people to share their stories in one or another of the Dialogue Circle sessions, and even specifically request it of them, "Be sure to include this or that part of your story when you tell us about it." The questions I ask the participants during the interview provide an opportunity for me to observe their reactions to the topic. The Pre–Dialogue

Circle interview also gives participants a chance to ask me questions, prior to meeting, about the Dialogue Circle and what will be discussed.

At the end of this chapter are a list of questions I use in conducting these interviews. I still conduct individual interviews for Dialogue Circle group members whenever possible.

Because many of my colleagues were aware of this project when I first started it, and the need to recruit participants for my pilot studies, people in different divisions of the agency made referrals. From among these, I selected individuals based upon participant interest in the topic and whether they were willing to sign on for the Dialogue Circle, making a personal commitment of time and energy. Ultimately, all participants were selected on a volunteer basis. My pilot groups included Caucasian, African American, American Indian, and Hispanic participants.

In each group, these participants fell into four categories: (1) senior level managers who had not had a TLE nor supervised any returning TLE employees; (2) senior level managers who had a traumatic experience and had supervised returning TLE employees; (3) senior level managers who had not had a traumatic experience but who had supervised at least one returning TLE employee; and, (4) TLE employees who had made a successful reentry to their workplace environment.

It is suggested, but not required, that the facilitator of the Dialogue Circle interview all named participants prior to the Dialogue Circle sessions. Usually interviewing is necessary in an organization where recently there has been intense trauma elsewhere in the country such as the Oklahoma bombing, post office shootings, or terrorist attacks. Immediately after such events, anxiety is high everywhere and managers and employees may feel ambivalent about returning to work, even half a continent away from the traumatic event. Pre-session interviews, especially at these times, can help participants become comfortable with the facilitator and the ambiance of the proposed Dialogue Circle.

In general, the interview makes the facilitator aware of the kinds of traumas participants have experienced and their comfort level in talking about them. If an organization chooses not to do the Pre–Dialogue Circle interviews, the Dialogue Circle will still be effective.

Helpful Tips

Prior to beginning the Dialogue Circle, participants should be given printed materials to read—a page or two—explaining the Dialogue Circle process and the roles of participants and facilitator.

Before each session participants should receive handout materials about the topic theme prior to each session. These handouts serve as reference for definitions of terms and questions for discussions. Participants appreciate having these handouts at least a few days before the session so they can mull over the questions in the meantime.

Each Dialogue Circle consists of three two-hour sessions. In my pilot groups, each session ran across the lunch hour, from 11:30 a.m. to 1:30 p.m. This proved to be an excellent time, convenient for both senior managers and other employees. In most cases, in a workplace setting a brown bag lunch is appropriate. My office provided a boxed lunch for each participant. Sharing lunch together at 11:30 served as a social warm-up for everyone and, in its own way, provided an incentive for the participants to share their experiences in the group. In most cases, by noon people were ready and eager to begin the session even before they had finished eating.

The sessions were held in an available seminar room in our building which offered easy access to all participants, few distractions, and lack of noise. I found it helpful to schedule Dialogue Circle sessions one week apart to give participants an opportunity to digest and, if possible, practice what they learned.

In general, sessions should be held in the workplace building, perhaps in a large conference room with ample space for individuals to move around in comfort. For this Dialogue Circle, the maximum group size is fifteen individuals; the minimum is eight. This guarantees rich and varied input. Ask participants to sit in a circle so that each person can see the faces of all others.

Getting Started

To get the discussion started, I usually begin by posing questions to the participants and inviting responses. I continue this approach throughout the session. This helps keep the discussion focused on the session's theme. As you watch a group deal with a question, the power of the Dialogue Circle's collaborative learning environment quickly becomes clear. The discussion is driven primarily by participant needs and interests. As participants share their experiences, learning occurs. You can see the lights going on in peoples' minds. Each person hears the experiences of other group members and relates it to their personal situation.

In the first session of one Dialogue Circle I led, I told Gwen's story and asked, if Gwen had been a coworker of theirs, how they would have put out a welcome mat for her? One participant said that when we had been discussing the *concept* of the welcome mat, he thought it would be very easy to design a generic welcome mat package in the workplace for any returning traumatized employee, and there would be no need for a Dialogue Circle on that idea. But after he heard Gwen's story, he realized such a generic package wouldn't be so easy to design, as she had lots of emotional assumptions going on inside her that her coworkers couldn't know about and might never know about until she told them. And since she was probably not ready to tell them what she was thinking and feeling about herself, her fellow employees would be hard pressed to come up with sure-fire suggestions for creating a safe haven.

As soon as this man stopped talking, people began realizing how each returning TLE employee has a unique personality, so there could be no set formula for creating a welcoming ceremony that would work for everyone. It had to be designed to fit each personality and each trauma.

And someone added, "But Gwen had really changed her self-image between the time she left work the previous Tuesday and the day she returned the follow week. She went home on Tuesday feeling like a happy and successful wife and she returned, though we didn't know it at the time, like a sad failure of a wife. So, which Gwen are we supposed to put out the welcome mat for?"

And would the unique safe haven we created for Gwen also work for the women who return to work after being raped or robbed on the street or whose car was hijacked? Or will it work for the employee whose spouse has a heart attack? Or for an employee diagnosed with a terminal illness? Or one whose mother suddenly dies?

The problem of employees returning to the workplace after a TLE has become increasingly urgent both to managers and coworkers, requiring that they possess both a theoretical and practical grasp of the issue. Theoretically, the Dialogue Circle introduces participants to the concepts of understanding the emotional recovery of trauma and the process that reentry employees will be going through. Practically, it teaches them how to talk and interact with TLE employees in such a way that the healing process is helped, not hindered.

Overview of a First Session

1. *Invite introductions.* I begin the Dialogue Circle's first session by having all the participants sit around a table or in a circle and introduce themselves. It's important to ask each participant to identify the specific division or branch that they are working in. This helps identify the organizational setting.

2. *Explain ground rules.* I then discuss the facilitator role and the importance of keeping the Dialogue Circle discussion focused. I explain to the group not to be afraid of conflicting issues that may come to the surface, and I encourage participants to engage in active dialogue. I also remind them of confidentiality as a protection for everyone concerned.

3. *Discuss topic.* I emphasize to the group the fact of their commitment to the topic being discussed and their desire to learn more about it. If the participants have strong feelings about the topic, this is generally good because it increases participation. I find it helpful to have a list of questions for discussion specific to each session. This helps me keep the discussion moving and focused. In general, I found individuals much more verbal and open to sharing during the Dialogue Circle sessions than they were during my interview with them.

4. *Summarize points.* I encourage participants to engage one another, to share their points of view and probe for more answers when an explanation may not seem clear. I watch for patterns of insight or key points that may occur during the group discussion and summarize those for the participants.

5. *Evaluate the session.* After a session but before we leave the room, I like to talk to the group about the learning process, find out what they liked and did not like during the session, and how the process could be improved. I learned that, before the group disperses, I need to remind participants about reading the handout and mulling over the discussion questions before the next Dialogue Circle session.

The Facilitator Role

The facilitator does not have to possess expert knowledge on the topic of the Dialogue Circle; however, he or she must be familiar enough with the subject matter to guide the participants through each session. If an organization chooses to have the facilitator conduct Pre–Dialogue Circle interviews, the facilitator will also gain firsthand knowledge of each individual's trauma experience. If pre-dialogue interviews are not conducted, the Dialogue Circle can move along as planned. The facilitator may simply need to be more observant, sensitive, and creative.

These are a few points important for a facilitator to remember when guiding a session.

1. *Understand group process.* Remember that your group will be composed of many different personalities who may share different values. Usu-

ally, each group forms its own group culture and develops its own timing and style for sharing thoughts, feelings, and experiences with each other. It's important to keep the group focused on the content of the subject matter. As a facilitator, you will learn that natural "moments of silence" at times may be good for the group, allowing them to process their thoughts, questions, and ideas.

2. *Set a participative tone.* As participants enter the meeting room, be sure to welcome each one and personally encourage them to participate. If this Dialogue Circle is one where a sensitive subject will be addressed, the facilitator should remember to allow participants to be themselves, and assure them that their experiences will add to the group dialogue.

3. *Work with Content.* It's important for the facilitator to focus on the topic and foster a lively exchange between members of the group. Asking probing, but open-ended questions and referring to specific discussion questions is the best way of getting others to participate and staying focused.

4. *Discuss questions.* Well-focused discussion questions handed out before each session can reduce pressure on the facilitator immensely. If such questions are printed in the session handout, they serve as a reference both for the participants and the facilitator.

5. *Close the discussion.* When the topic has been discussed sufficiently, the facilitator takes the initiative to ask the group whether anything has been missed during the group exchange.

6. *Summarize the session.* To remind participants of what they have learned during this session, the facilitator might ask questions like:
   a. What thoughts are you leaving this Dialogue Circle with today?
   b. When you return to the workplace, will you feel more confident in dealing with a returning TLE? Why?
   c. Will you be able to share some of your concerns with others?
   d. What did you learn today that you can use practically?

Facilitators Sharing Their Own Trauma Stories

Facilitators can be especially effective if they personally had a TLE or have supervised an individual who reentered the workplace after having one. Although prior personal experience of a trauma is not required, the facilitator's sensitivity and ability to share such a personal experience in the group sets a tone for sharing. It presents an invitation and gives permission for others to share their stories.

For example, in the Dialogue Circle's second session I often begin by sharing my trauma story with the group—the death of my father. I would tell them not merely the facts surround his death, but also what went on inside me when it happened. I would tell them that my father had been a friend and mentor to me all through my career, someone I could always lean on and count on. When he died, I felt like I had lost one of my arms. I described how I felt off balance; as though I would have to relearn how to stand up straight and how to do things I was used to doing but now with one arm missing. "In a way," I would explain, "I had to reorient my whole life." Telling your story models for participants how they might begin to tell of their own TLEs. Soon afterward, other members begin to share their own stories and a new level of interaction and trust emerges. As a facilitator, telling a personal story enables other participants to feel a level of comfort. It also sets the tone for further openness, encouraging other participants to retell their trauma experiences.

In a Dialogue Circle the role of the facilitator is unique and should not be confused with leaders in other types of group work. For example, often a Dialogue Circle facilitator is inaccurately described as a mediator. At the outset, the two facilitating roles may seem similar, but their objectives are totally different. In mediation, parties in disagreement are brought together to negotiate a settlement and resolve a conflict. This is not so in a Dialogue Circle. There is no disagreement to be negotiated. People are coming together to learn from each other. The main task for the facilitator in a Dialogue Circle is to assist and improve the group process and help people develop more effective interpersonal behavior as this learning happens.

Sample Material for Facilitators

Letter of Invitation for Participants

Dear Participant,
I would like to invite you to participate in a Dialogue Circle titled "Helping Managers and Coworkers Deal with an Employee Returning to the Workplace after a Traumatic Life Experience (TLE)."

I have long been professionally interested in creating positive work environments. Organizations today are continually faced with the issue of effectively assimilating traumatized employees who are returning to their jobs. Dealing with such individuals poses a unique dilemma to organizations and, in particular, to managers and coworkers who have the responsibility of assisting such returning survivors to make the reentry transition as smoothly, effectively, and quickly as possible. Many managers and coworkers have little or no idea how best to do this, mostly because they do not understand the stages of emotional recovery that a traumatized person will normally go through. This Dialogue Circle is designed to fill that gap.

A Dialogue Circle is a specially designed form of adult education that has been used successfully for over one hundred years. It is especially effective in dealing with sensitive issues of interest to participants. During Dialogue Circle sessions complex issues are broken down into manageable discussion points and controversial topics are discussed in depth.

In this Dialogue Circle, about eight to twelve people will meet for three sessions. Each session will last for no more than two hours. Participants will be a mix of managers and employees in the group. I will discuss with each participant the scheduling of the Dialogue Circle sessions. It is important that you participate in all three sessions.

The proposed schedule is:

Session	Theme	Date	Time	Location
1.	Putting out a Welcome Mat			
2.	Lending a Listening Ear			
3.	Offering a Helping Hand			

One of the best aspects of the Dialogue Circles is that expertise on the topic under discussion is not necessary. Rather, Dialogue Circles are a learning format through which people like you and me can bring the experience of ordinary people to bear on important workplace issues. All you need is a willingness to participate in the discussions and to really want to hear what others have to say. I can promise you the discussions will be spirited, cordial, and informative and—best of all—fun!

I will contact you in a few days to discuss any questions you may have and deliver materials for our first Dialogue Circle session. If you have any questions, please call me.

Sincerely,

Confidentiality Agreement
I, [Participant], as a condition of a participant in the Dialogue Circle session for "Helping Managers and Coworkers Deal with an Employee Returning to the Workplace after a Traumatic Like Experience (TLE)," being facilitated by [Your Name] at [Location] on [Dates] hereby agree that I will not, directly or indirectly, divulge or otherwise make known to any person or entity any personal and confidential information of any type disclosed by other participants during the course of the said Dialogue Circle.

I understand that any personal and confidential information in nature disclosed by participants in the Dialogue Circle sessions is to remain personal and confidential, and that any personal and confidential information that I may provide during the course of the Dialogue Circle will be treated as such by all other participants each of whom will be required to sign a Confidentiality Statement identical to this one as a condition of their participation in the Dialogue Circle sessions.

Facilitator' Signature　　　　　　　　*Participant's Signature*
Date　　　　　　　　　　　　　　　*Date*

Pre–Dialogue Circle Interview Questions

Some of these interview questions may be used by the facilitator prior to the Dialogue Circle sessions to interview managers and employees. Let the organization and the facilitator discern whether Pre–Dialogue Circle interviews should be carried out.

The following questions are suggested to explore a participant's experience and understanding of TLEs and their effects in the workplace. These are questions I generally ask of participants during interviews prior to the first Dialogue Circle session:

1. Did you ever have a personal experience with trauma? If so, how did you handle it? What was your experience in returning to work afterward?
2. Did you ever have a coworker who experienced a trauma and returned to the workplace? What did you say to that person when they returned? How did you treat that person?
3. If an employee were returning to the workplace today after having experienced a trauma, how would you behave toward that person? Have your ideas about treating such a person changed over time?
4. Have you ever observed an employee talking with a coworker and sharing their trauma story upon their return to the workplace?
5. Would you normally ask a returning employee to tell of their traumatic experience or share their story upon returning to the workplace?
6. How comfortable do you feel approaching or talking to a person who has just returned to work after having experienced a trauma?
7. Do you know what things to say to a returning TLE employee that will help them feel welcome when they return to work?
8. How would you go about assisting the returning TLE employee to participate in office activities?
9. How would you respond to a TLE employee who refuses to work and begins to have emotional outbursts?

10. Do you think gender plays a role in dealing with a returning TLE employee? Do women behave differently from men in this regard when they return to the workplace?

Manager only questions:

1. Did you ever supervise a person who returned to the workplace after having experienced a trauma? If so, how did you handle it?
2. What approach would you use if you had to communicate your expectations to a person on their first day back to work after having experienced a trauma?
3. How would you go about explaining to your staff the importance of greeting and talking with the person who is returning to the workplace after their trauma?
4. What would you do if you had to set limits with a returning TLE employee when he or she returns to work? For example, if the person started coming to work consistently late.
5. How would you present work assignments and expectations of productivity to the returning TLE employee?

It is important that you ask these questions gently and openly, not as if they were a test to be passed for keeping one's job or for future employment assignments.

~

CHAPTER TEN

Putting Out a Welcome Mat

The First Dialogue Circle

Interactive Learning

In working with and training adults over the past twenty years, I have concluded, along with many practitioners of adult education, that adults learn best through interactive forms of education. When you bring adults together to discuss a sensitive topic, which they all share and about which they have strong feelings, it proves to be a powerful educational force. Because of the Dialogue Circle's interactive nature, participants during the sessions discover themselves as part of a new and intimate group culture that they themselves create.

Because each Dialogue Circle finds its own pace and rhythm, it's hard to predict what will happen when a diverse group of people come together to discuss an emotionally charged topic. However, you can be sure it will be interesting, lively, and transforming. And, as evidenced from the continuous interactive involvement of all the participants, the process consistently proves very beneficial.

In each of the three Dialogue Circle sessions, participants explore what is needed in an organization so managers and employees can help understand the emotional recovery process in a returning traumatized employee. The first session focuses on *putting out a welcome mat* for the returning TLE employee; the second centers around *lending a listening ear* to understanding how retelling the trauma experience story can influence emotional recovery; and in the third, *offering a helping hand*, participants seek to find ways to help TLE employees reconnect to the workplace.

Getting Started

Before each session, each participant is given a handout describing the theme to be discussed during the Dialogue Circle session plus some questions to stimulate dialogue. For example, for the "welcome mat" session, participants mulled over questions like the following:

"What would it take to put out a welcome mat in your workplace environment for a returning TLE employee?"

"What would it look like and feel like if your workplace was emotionally 'unsafe' for a returning TLE employee?"

"In your workplace, what are some of the current typical reactions of people to returning TLE employees?"

"What kinds of questions might you ask the returning TLE employee to find out what would make them feel personally welcome?"

Usually when TLE employees return to the workplace, they are anxious and ambivalent about how they will be seen and treated by their coworkers, especially if their traumatic experience has kept them from work for an extended period of time. Consequently, they may be hesitant about immediately socializing with fellow employees and may feel they don't quite belong to the organization yet.

Outside work, they may be seeing a social worker or therapist for grief work or depression, and may be taking medication that affects their ability to focus. Because of this, they may act strangely or impetuously on the job. They may feel emotionally unsafe or embarrassed among their coworkers, as they tend not to have their customary control over their emotions and reactions.

Some returning TLE employees are not sure how to behave in workplace situations where previously they had acted with confidence. Someone else has obviously been doing their job while they were home or hospitalized, and they wonder if the person who temporarily replaced them will be doing so permanently.

Because they probably also have difficulty sleeping at night and concentrating during the day, this may manifest itself at work as an inability to complete tasks they could easily do before the traumatic experience. After a trauma, some may want to go into seclusion and hide from others. Their old reality seems broken and nothing feels solid or certain anymore.

Managers and coworkers are often confused and uncomfortable in relating to TLE employees when they first return to work.

What Does It Mean to Put Out a Welcome Mat?

As participants in the first session discuss feelings of security with the return-ing TLE employees, the question naturally arises about the types of welcome mats a traumatized person might need. The obvious way to begin is to ask TLE survivors in the group what their managers and coworkers could have done to make the workplace a safe haven to come back to after their TLE.

Each group will probably put a different meaning on a "welcome mat" that provides safety and security. One group might list things like financial assis-tance or support from the organization, time off that may be needed for psycho-logical readjustments, flexibility with work assignments, empathy, and trust.

Another group, taking a different approach, might want to identify the natural welcoming gestures that already exist in organizations, such as ongo-ing friendships at the workplace, the natural and spontaneous bonding that occurs between colleagues, managers, and supervisors.

A third group, feeling that the task of creating a safe haven falls primar-ily upon managers, might aim their advice at the manager saying what they think he or she should do upon the TLE employees' return. This is a common turn Dialogue Circle groups sometimes take in the first session, especially because managers do not always know what to say, and few of them may be willing to admit it. Here is a short summary of advice one group gave managers:

- Let the TLE employee set the pace. Follow the flow of the employee.
- Express empathy toward the returning TLE employee.
- Remember that when individuals return to the workplace they want normalcy as much as you do but they realize it won't happen immedi-ately and certainly not without your help.

Many managers may find it difficult to follow TLE employees' advice, but those who are trauma survivors agree that the company would have gotten more from them if managers had taken the lead from the survivors.

As for "expressing empathy," the group's second recommendation, it is much easier said than done. Few of us are in the habit of expressing empathy, because it begins with a special kind of empathic listening. According to Karla McLaren in *The Art of Empathy: A Complete Guide to Life's Most Es-sential Skill*, empathy is developed in interactions. The quality of your current interactions, she says, has a large impact on your empathic capacities. If you have shallow relationships or inattentive friends and family members, and if your relationships are not fulfilling, your empathic abilities may languish.

On the other hand, she adds, if your relationships are deep and satisfying, if you have family members and friends who can meet you where you are and can understand you, if your emotional styles are compatible, if your emotion workloads are equal, and if you have other healthy empaths in your life, then your empathic abilities will most likely flourish. Empathy is developed in interactions, and you can increase and deepen your empathic abilities at any point in your life.[1]

McLaren stresses the point of "learning people intentionally." Here she explains the importance of studying body language and facial expressions, and how learning these skills can help you develop your empathic ability. For example, when you are conversing with someone or counseling someone, your simplest gestures send a message, for instance, when you "raise your eyebrows" or "you look surprised"—you are engaging another person to confirm or correct your impression. You are asking, "Is that what is going on?" "Did I pick that up correctly?" or "Is that how you're feeling?"[2] Such a simple gesture qualifies as an interaction, and other people respond to it. And "that's the magic."

Empathic listening is not a skill someone learns merely wishing for it. It takes practice built upon a strong compassion for others. This is a challenge for managers.

In one discussion about expressing empathy to the returning TLE employee, managers in a Dialogue Circle session pointed out that, though empathic listening sounds like a great approach, they face a very complex issue because, besides going through an emotional recovery process, survivors are simultaneously facing managers with performance issues and behavioral problems. Some returning TLE employees are uncommunicative, while others can't stop talking or are rebellious and disruptive—even destructive. Some refuse to work, while others work sloppily or make many mistakes. Some are unforgiving, while others are busy punishing themselves. How does a manager show empathy, yet still run an effective workplace?

The third recommendation focused on the survivor's wish for a "return to normalcy." This is, of course, what everyone wishes for. But the workplace situation with a newly returning TLE is not "normal." And, to most managers, the path to normalcy is unknown and unpredictable. Besides, the path to normalcy may take different twists and turns for each returning survivor.

A Larger Perspective

The idea of putting out a welcome mat for returning TLE employees reflects a very basic human need. The psychologist Abraham Maslow identified a pyramid of five basic need levels, without which a full human life cannot be lived. At the base of the pyramid, the most fundamental of all needs are the physical and physiological ones, such as air, water, food, clothing, shelter, and the touch of another human being. Without all of these, a person would soon get sick and might even die. This first need level is essential and a requirement for all the other ones in the pyramid of needs.

The next level includes the needs Maslow described as "safety and security" needs. Unless a person feels safe and secure, no matter how plentifully their physical needs are met, they remain anxious and fearful for their life, health, and well-being. We are a nation preoccupied with safety and security. Not only are our homes locked, bolted, and secured, but the possessions in them are insured against flood, fire, wind, rain, and theft. We take out insurance for liability, disability, health care, hospitalization, retirement, and long-term care. We have national programs for Social Security and Medicare. We also feel the need to be safe and secure wherever we happen to be—in our homes, our cars, shopping malls, elevators, airports, and the building where we work.

While physical safety at work is of primary importance so that no harm comes to our bodies, emotional safety is also important to us. One who is unwelcome in a certain place is not likely to feel emotionally safe there. Being greeted with scowls, giggles, or worst of all, indifference does not make one feel safe. Often, Dialogue Circle participants can easily begin the first session by identifying ways they could make returning TLE employees feel *unsafe*. From these examples, they begin to recognize what *not* to do to help with the recovery process from a TLE.

You can't expect returning workers to begin directing their efforts for the company in creative efficient and effective ways until they feel safe and secure in the workplace. Until emotional and financial safety is assured, the employee, consciously or unconsciously, will be testing to see whether the office environment is "safe." There is a simple rule about human energy that says *energy follows attention*. Wherever your attention is focused, that's where your energy will be directed. If you are frightened or feel insecure, your energy will be primarily directed at self-protection and safety and not at the work that needs to get done.

Almost all managers in the Dialogue Circle I have facilitated agree that there are two essential factors in providing safety—one emotional and one financial—that, if provided would go far to reduce stress for any returning TLE employees. One part of a "welcome mat" protects emotional safety by providing a place where TLE employees could be and no one would force their way into someone's private feelings. The other part was the assured continuance of their salary or wages.

Notice that this financial "welcome mat" assures the employee that physical needs, the most basic need of all according to Maslow, will be covered: there will be enough money to pay the bills for food, water, clothing shelter, and medicines. The emotional "welcome mat" begins to cover what Maslow call the need for safety and security.

But, aside from these two provisions, most managers shake their heads and wonder what other good things they can do for the employees in their charge. That's where the Dialogue Circle proves its value.

Conflicting Values

Observations from the first session show that some managers hesitate to take responsibility for returning TLE employees. As far as they are concerned, caring for TLE employees' recovery is someone else's job. Some managers realize they can send the TLE employees to EAP or to a professional counselor for therapy. Once they have made the professional referral, some managers feel that they have taken care of their responsibility.

In one Dialogue Circle, some participant managers said they hesitated to get involved with TLE employees on an emotional level. They claimed they did not have the professional skills to help, they did not want to interfere with the therapist's work, and they felt that the amount of hands-on time needed to nurture the employee back to normal would jeopardize other work assignments that had to be completed.

However, in the second session of that Dialogue Circle, I presented each one in the group with a photocopied page of "notes from the previous session." After reading the notes about putting out a welcome mat, the group quickly clarified a short list of what others in the workplace could do for returning TLE employees. Most of the items on that list would take very little time to do yet would still be very helpful.

During the first Dialogue Circle session on creating a welcome mat for the returning TLE employees, managers typically acknowledge having two colliding values, one that favors compassion, and the other that favors productivity. On the one hand, managers say, "We are responsible for the 'bottom line' and getting the work done. So, even though we feel concern for the traumatized person, we are conflicted about spending precious work time tending to a TLE employee."

After a first session, one employee told me how amazed he was that managers were making such a hard call on performance for a returning TLE employee. He had personally experienced a very uncomfortable transition upon his return to his job. "Because of my trauma, it was very difficult to concentrate on my work when I returned," he said. "Fortunately, I didn't have the kind of manager who got on my back about work quotas." I encouraged this young man to share his views with the group during the next session, if and when he felt comfortable.

Usually, all the managers attending a Dialogue Circle agree that, at first, returning TLE employees should be "acknowledged" when they return to the workplace. Once, a TLE survivor in the Dialogue Circle responded to such a remark by saying, "Acknowledgment is good, but we survivors need more than that. Use common sense. Treat us as you would like to be treated if you were in our shoes."

After the first session, two of the male managers and a female employee were demonstrating to each other how they relate to their returning TLE employees. They said that when it's appropriate they like to give a hug to people when they welcome them back to the workplace. They chose to be demonstrative and touching.

How Could They Know?

Most managers feel unsure how to approach returning TLE employees. This is no surprise because no one has ever told them how to do it in a way designed to be helpful to the trauma survivor's emotional recovery. Whatever managers did, helpful or unhelpful, they did intuitively.

When I was doing my doctoral research on the topic of traumatized employees and how they fared when returning to their jobs, I found almost nothing in the professional literature, other than how therapists were learning to deal with clients suffering from posttraumatic stress. What could be done in the workplace by managers and coworkers to understand the emotional recovery from the trauma appeared to be an unexplored area. That is why I am writing about what I learned and experimented with. I want to fill in the missing place in the care of traumatized people who find themselves back at work, yet still in the process of healing and adjusting.

During the Dialogue Circle sessions, managers almost universally express a need for guidance on how to tell the coworkers about the returning TLE employees, how they themselves are to negotiate with the TLE employees about work assignments, and how to create a workplace environment that is nonthreatening for the returning employees.

A few years ago, a civil rights manager in my office told me that he received a phone call from a director of a government agency, reporting that some of his employees were experiencing a variety of traumatic life events and that he, their director, felt helpless in not having any program available to help his line managers cope with returning TLE employees. The civil rights manager in my department said he shared his Dialogue Circle experiences with the agency director and was pleased to be able to offer suggestions to him.

Many managers of large corporations or organizations agree that their enterprise probably has many professional resources such as training counselors and workshops available to returning TLE employees. However, managers are often not aware of the extent of these programs. They would probably agree that an informational program should be officially provided so that managers know how to ensure that employees get the best available professional assistance when they are dealing with recovery from traumatic incidents.

Here is a sketch of one Dialogue Circle participant named Winston. It is the story of a powerful manager and how he learned about workplace trauma.

Winston's Personality

Winston volunteered to participate in the Dialogue Circle session even though he had never experienced personal trauma. During my Pre–Dialogue Circle interview with him, his only recollection of anything like a traumatic experience was secondhand and it happened with predictable regularity. His wife came from a very close family, and when they returned home from a visit to her family home in South Carolina, it would take her days to readjust to life without them. It was "traumatic," he said, "for her to leave them."

Winston is a large man, forty-five, an African American with an effervescent personality. He has black wavy hair and his wardrobe is the envy of every other manager in the entire company. He is stylish in every sense of the word and his style matches his extroverted personality. He wears pastel shirts with cuff links and always has a silver bracelet on his right wrist. This bracelet holds much personal significance for him, since he bought it in Mexico and watched as the silversmith created it for him.

Winston was born in 1951 in Alabama in a town about thirty miles south of Mobile. Because his dad was in the army, they moved around a lot and he considered himself an army brat. Winston thrived on the variety, stating, "Every three years I had a new home, new experiences and met new people. It was an adventure." However, he spent the longest time in the Norfolk, Virginia, area, where he returned to work as an adult.

His parents have been very influential in his life. He describes his father as organized and conscientious, his mother as outgoing and someone who makes friends easily. His mother's keen sense of style, fashion, and skill helped her establish her own business in cosmetology. Although she was not formally trained, she ran her business from their home successfully. Her friendliness always did well for her. Winston described his mother as a "really classy person." Like his mother, he exudes friendliness and is consequently very well liked in his department. Winston has two sisters and a brother. One sister lives in Baltimore, Maryland, the other in California, and his brother lives in Charlotte, North Carolina. He was a middle child.

When you meet Winston, he seems "larger than life." He spends a lot of time on the phone negotiating and talking with colleagues and the general public. His supervisor suggested that I invite Winston to participate in a Dialogue Circle I was facilitating near Norfolk, Virginia. When I approached Winston, he agreed to come, even before I could explain what the Dialogue Circle would entail. During the sessions, he was often the first to speak out and get others involved in a dialogue about the topic. He affirmed employees whenever they shared their trauma stories or took the risk of asking managers sensitive questions about their own personal traumas.

In the Dialogue Circle, he played the role of catalyst and everyone seemed to respond to his disarming manner. He loved to challenge, ask questions, and propose taking a different path to a solution. He was the only manager who outwardly disagreed with the group's consensus on topics. Surprisingly, instead of setting people in opposition, this created more energy in the Dialogue Circle, because the group then seemed to participate in a more active manner by asking new questions and probing for more information.

Winston started his career with a large government agency as a Budget Officer, then soon moved into a position that spanned several government agencies. He considers himself a policeman for his agency's budget process. He is asked to do things others do not want to do. When his mentor retired, he applied for his job and got it. He has been in his present job since 1998.

Winston has three children—a daughter Penny from his first marriage and two sons from his second marriage, Pelman and Price. His current wife decided to quit her job when she married Winston, to be a stay-at-home mother. When I asked about the divorce from his first marriage, Winston said he did not consider it a trauma. I wondered if there were other traumas in his past.

In 1976 when Winston was a teen, his family moved from Kansas to the Navy base in Norfolk, Virginia. Winston was to be part of the first group to be integrated into the nearby high school. Out of 1,500 students in the school only five were African American—a natural setting for some traumatic experiences. He was in the eleventh grade at this time, he said, and adjusted very well. He joined the basketball and football teams in twelfth grade and became co-captain of both teams. He states that he still goes to reunions with his friends and they talk about how it felt to all of them to handle the issue of integration. Winston says he is not intimidated by racism. "It exists, and we as a people and a society should deal with it."

Winston's Experience in the Dialogue Circle

As the only one in the circle who had not experienced a personal trauma, Winston said he truly felt blessed compared to people who had no choice in the way some terrible events unfolded in their lives. Winston said he knows of people who just give up, but he proudly announced he did not observe anyone in the Dialogue Circle who had done this. He told participants in the Dialogue Circle they were his heroes, because they had not walked away from their trauma and pain, he said, but had become better people for it.

I watched Winston as other people were telling their trauma stories. He remained quiet and pensive, almost reverent. One employee, Jim, described being part of the Long Island Train disaster of 1993, where a deranged man stood in the aisle of a passenger car and shot bullets in every direction. Telling us the story, Jim said he crawled under the seat and, in complete shock, stayed there until the shooting stopped and police came. Winston was the first person to ask Jim questions as to how he felt when he returned to the workplace as a TLE employee. This question allowed Jim to elaborate his feelings in detail, which stimulated the dialogue among the rest of the participants.

Winston told the group that he had watched the trial of that shooter on television and could, even today, describe the event on that train in graphic details, but when he realized that he was hearing an eyewitness report in the Dialogue Circle, this overwhelmed him. While watching the trial on television, Winston said, he had gotten very angry at the shooter and wished him dead. But how he said he admired Jim retelling his terrifying experience without any malice for the man who almost killed him. Jim's story had a strong impact on Winston. He felt the Dialogue Circle group had allowed him to see beyond his own situation in life. The group gave him "balance" in his thinking, and that was refreshing to him.

Winston's Experience with Trauma after the First Dialogue Circle Session

During the week between the first and second Dialogue Circle sessions, one of Winston's employee's came to him and told him she had cancer. He could tell she was traumatized by this unexpected announcement from her doctor. The situation was confusing to Winston, because this same person had recently filed an EEO complaint against him, and he did not know what to do about it. Winston was faced with an inner conflict that had to be resolved. He approached the situation, as he told us at the next session, in a "clinical manner." He felt that the EEO complaint was going to be resolved by the standard procedures within the system, and he was ready to accept the decision that the system would give him.

However, dealing with the traumatized employee was totally different. It was something new for him. Winston said that he remembered the suggestions and ideas he had learned from the Dialogue Circle's first session. He tried to put out a welcome mat for her by allowing her the necessary leave for her treatment. He assured her he was there for her if she wanted to talk and would do all that he could for her in this crisis.

Winston said the discussion in the Dialogue Circle helped him take a caring approach in dealing with his returning TLE employee. He had listened to other participants talking about their supervisors and their often-thoughtless treatment of traumatized employees and, as a result, he had become more sensitive to his TLE employee with cancer. Up to this point, he had always been a bottom-line manager concerned with productivity and output, so he seldom allowed people to get extensions on work assignments. Now, with his newly learned attitudes, he was confronted with a totally different situation, one with which he never had dealt, approving sick and annual leave in advance for someone who was really trying to hurt him as a manager. He said the Dialogue Circle put lot of these issues into perspective for him.

Winston said that the presence of employees in the Dialogue Circle helped him understand what the returning TLE was dealing with internally. Hearing employees share their trauma stories would help him put his workplace requirements in perspective and offer this TLE employee—and future ones—more of a welcome mat than he previously would have done.

Winston is an interesting personality study because he seems to be one of those people who pass through life untouched by TLEs. For example, while many military "brats" have been traumatized because of continual uprooting of their home life and friendship, Winston found frequent moves an adventure. Again, during the difficult times of racial integration, when many African American teens were traumatized by cruel treatment from whites in these schools, Winston seems to have passed through it all, not merely unscathed but coming out on top as co-captain of two varsity sports teams. And again, when one of his employees filed an EEO complaint against him—his first, by the way—he could have experienced this as a TLE, and many in his position would have, but he did not.

As I mentioned in an earlier chapter, psychologists have noticed that people who have adversely responded to traumatic events early in life are more likely to be traumatized by potentially traumatizing events in adult life than people, like Winston, who had not been traumatized by events in childhood. The point is that when different people are faced with the same potentially traumatizing event, one may be traumatized by it while the other may not. One becomes a returning TLE employee who needs help and support through recovery, the other is simply an employee who has had to face a difficult situation and becomes a better person for it.

Instead of being brought down traumatically by the EEO complaint against him, Winston seemed more concerned with helping the woman readjust to the workplace. He did not brush off the hurt that her complaint brought him. It was simply something difficult for him to deal with. But it was not a trauma for him. Interestingly, what he found more challenging was discovering ways to understand the emotional recovery process for the woman. After the Dialogue Circle, Winston became concerned about the three stages of her emotional recovery that were discussed in the Dialogue Circle—not about the cancer itself, which he could do nothing about, but about the trauma of the announcement of it and the changes it had brought about in her sense of self.

Winston says, "It is difficult coping with my TLE employee with cancer. I did okay with the welcome mat thing, but I can't seem to completely reconnect her to the workforce. I don't know what to do. I have tried to talk with her about her trauma, but she refuses to discuss anything with me. I think she has come back to the workplace with a victim mentality. My employee has cancer but also because she has not resolved the issues that made her bring the EEO complaint against me."

Regarding the complaint, which he feels is unfounded, he says, "I've got to put the past behind me and move forward. But, thanks to the Dialogue Circle, I can at least help this woman put her trauma in perspective and become a better person for it."

An Element of Policy Awareness

The Dialogue Circle can serve as a healthy catalyst for a manager's attitude toward a returning TLE employee. The manager is typically the first person to greet trauma survivors when they return to the workplace, and the manager plays a key role in forming a good relationship with that person upon their reentry. It is here, on the first day back, when the manager can derail a potential adverse action or grievance. The manager who establishes good communication patterns will eliminate unnecessary performance problems with the reentry employee. By giving the returning TLE employee a listening ear and acknowledging his return, this type of behavior will create strong credibility with an employee and help the emotional recovery process. Here are a few suggestions that Winston's group offered:

- Acknowledge the TLE employees' presence when they come back to work. A suggested greeting might be, "I am glad you're back to work. How are things with you? What can I do to help you?"
- Offer a listening ear. Show the returning TLE employees that you are interested by practicing active listening skills.
- Body language plays an important part. Watch for behavioral cues from the returning employees, and watch your own behavioral signals. One negative gesture from you will nullify all your compassionate words.
- If TLE employees do not want to talk to the managers, suggest that they talk to a colleague or someone at work that they trust.

Some Dos and Don'ts

After years of conducting Dialogue Circles on understanding emotional recovery from trauma and from reading many related books, I have developed a list of dos and don'ts in dealing with survivors of trauma who return to the workplace to start their work lives over. Some of these suggestions have already been mentioned, but I thought it helpful to put them together in one place. Studies show that traumatized people often benefit most from talking with family and friends. As Sheryle Baker, former director of the Life Center of the Suncoast, Tampa, Florida, mental health counselor and trauma expert, says about recovery from trauma, "It all begins with a conversation." Here are some of the best ways to reach out to returning TLE employees:

Dos

- Reassure them they are good people and that you care about them.
- Show them that you care by hugging them or holding their hand.
- Sit with them quietly and show empathy—your presence is important.
- Share your own feelings (not opinions) about the traumatic experience.
- Be prepared to just listen and say nothing.
- Allow them to go through their grieving process at their own pace.
- Encourage them to take advantage of assistance services.

Don'ts

- Don't avoid them or leave them feeling abandoned.
- Don't be afraid to ask how they are doing.
- Don't invalidate their feelings by saying things like "Cheer up" or "Stop crying."
- Don't tell them to stop complaining and get on with their lives.
- Don't tell them they're lucky it wasn't worse.
- Don't take their expressions of anger or other strong reactions personally.
- Don't try to impose your own opinions about why the trauma happened.

Notes

1. Karla McLaren, *The Art of Empathy: A Complete Gide to Life's Most Essential Skill* (Boulder, CO: Sounds True, 2013), 183.

2. McLaren, *The Art of Empathy* 188–89.

CHAPTER ELEVEN

~

Lending a Listening Ear

The Second Dialogue Circle

Developing Sensitivity

A Dialogue Circle facilitator can never predict how individual participants will work together in a group setting or react to each other. All you can count on is that they will be interested in the topic of how to deal with employees returning to work after a TLE.

This second Dialogue Circle session, because of its topic, lending a listening ear, creates a bond among participants mainly since managers and employees alike have themselves experienced trauma and the difficulties with returning to work. And if they haven't experienced a traumatic life event personally, they have managed or worked beside someone who has. But even when participants, like Winston in the previous chapter, have neither experienced a trauma nor supervised a returning TLE employee, they will admit, like Winston, that the sessions "enhanced my sensitivity toward a traumatized employee."

Second Session

The theme of the second session in the Dialogue Circle on understanding the emotional recovery of trauma is *lending a listening ear*, for returning TLE employees to feel free to tell the trauma story and experience.

Some of the discussion questions proposed on the participant handout for this session are:

"What would it mean to you to 'lend a listening ear' to returning TLE
   employees who want to tell their trauma story?"
"Are there ways nonverbally, to 'not allow' such employees to tell their
   story, even if they wanted to?"
"Are there ways you could invite the victims to tell their trauma story that
   would *not* be helpful in the person's emotional recovery?"
"Do you know how to use 'active listening skills' with the TLE employee?"

Sometimes persons who have suffered a trauma have been so shocked by
it that they find it difficult to recall the event at all or they remember only
parts of it. Even when the trauma is vivid in their minds and even though it
would be psychologically helpful for them to talk about it, they are reluctant
to do so and find themselves avoiding people who would encourage them to
talk. After all, if you had been raped and beaten, would you be eager to talk
about it to coworkers? Or if your husband had run off with another woman
because he said he was bored with you, would you feel comfortable sharing
the details of your traumatic experience with the person who works at the
desk next to you? So, allowing and inviting traumatized employees to talk
about their traumatic experience is not a simple matter.

Some traumatized people are tempted to drink alcohol to ease their suffering. Others may turn to brooding and blaming themselves for the traumatic
incident. Depending on the trauma, survivors may feel degraded, shamed,
humiliated, helpless, isolated, in pain, fearful, anxious, angry, resentful, or
some other unwelcomed feeling. It is safe to say that there is probably much
emotional turbulence going on in returning TLE employees. They may need
to get it out somehow, hopefully in a nonharmful way. Talking it out with
the right kind of person almost always helps.

Respecting Personalities

In the second session, I find most participants are open and spontaneous.
I had one group in which participants during that session freely recounted
fourteen different traumatic stories. They told me about their trauma experiences, gave each other feedback, and shared their philosophy of life. They
discussed the importance of respecting an individual's personality and culture during the reentry process. They observed that some individuals were
introverts and some extroverts, and that this aspect of a person's personality
influenced whether they would be open to talking about their trauma.

They also recognized that some individuals may have been brought up
not to talk about personal matters to anyone outside their family. Such

people, they said, might not feel comfortable sharing an intimate side of their personality with a coworker. All participants agreed that, if returning TLE employees choose not to share their painful experiences, managers and coworkers should honor this wish. A listening ear is not a demanding ear.

In contrast, I once had a group who found it hard to focus on the telling of their own trauma stories, even though I began the session by telling about a trauma event in my own life. After I finished and no one spoke, I asked an employee participant to tell her trauma story. When she finished, the group complimented her. As part of her story, she said she had been grateful that, when she first returned to work after the event, her boss had encouraged her to talk about her traumatic event. The group affirmed her for risking, letting her story be known in the workplace and told her that her boss had excellent listening skills.

One participant, who sat across the table from her with his hands folded in a closed position, complimented her on her courage in telling her story. However, he did not offer to tell his story, which I knew was a powerful one, as he had told it to me during his Pre–Dialogue Circle interview. The focus on this group seemed to be not on telling their own trauma stories, but on how they believed managers should act responsibly in dealing with returning TLE employees. They seemed more focused on the political environment of the organization than on the individual's story.

You can never predict the direction a group will take: you can only be sure that it will be heartfelt and emotional. Their stories are.

Tony: A Case Study in the Effects of a Personal Trauma

Tony's story shows show how unaware our organizations are in general in understanding and dealing with individuals who have experienced a personal trauma in their family and are returning to the workplace. I watched how this manager tried to function in two worlds—his professional life and his personal family life—over a period of two years. I was able to observe Tony not only during Dialogue Circle sessions but also to listen to him reply to personal questions in an interview. Using this two-level observation process I followed his story from the beginning and gained new perspectives on trauma and some specific needs an individual has when he returns to the workplace.

The Organization and Tony's Place in It

Tony works as a senior officer in a government agency in a branch office in Cincinnati. The employees who work at this department represent America's full ethnic, social, cultural, religious, and educational diversity. The Midwest is the hub for all major social programs sponsored, funded, and overseen by the federal government.

Tony has been employed by the government for twenty-six years. He is a white Anglo male, fifty-two years old, medium height with light grayish brown hair. A handsome man, he sports a mustache and wears frameless glasses.

Tony was born and raised in Brooklyn, New York. His ancestry is Italian, and he speaks with a Brooklyn accent that contrasts with his Oxford button-down collar and navy blue blazer look. He was raised Roman Catholic and grew up in a big family with parents who placed a high value on hard work, education, and an active church and community commitment.

He came to Washington in the early 1960s, obtaining his first job with the Census Bureau. He also worked with a private corporation and relocated to the central part of the country. Once settled in Washington, he married Connie, his high school sweetheart, and together they raised five children. At the time I met Tony in Cincinnati, his oldest child was twenty-seven, his youngest sixteen.

Tony's World Turns Upside Down

Tony's trauma story began in August 1989, with a telephone call from Dr. Granger of the City Hospital in Cleveland, informing him that his daughter Melody, who was fifteen years old at the time, was diagnosed with cancer. Earlier that month, Melody had found some lumps near her collarbone and brought them to her parents' attention. After two weeks, they seemed to get larger. Tony took her for an examination, and a biopsy identified the cancer. The doctors performed an emergency laparotomy and splenectomy. The cancer had not spread, they said. She then began six months of chemotherapy treatments and ten days of radiation.

Upon hearing the diagnosis of his daughter Melody, Tony told me, his priorities immediately changed. No longer was he concerned about advancing his career and status or earning a lot of money. None of these any longer seemed important to him. His total focus was on his daughter and her well-being—and trying to figure out what to do. Like the good analyst that he was, Tony immediately began to research her illness through the available medical school libraries in his area. He even made trips to the National Institute of Health in Bethesda, Maryland. In a short time, he became an expert on her illness, her drugs, and her treatment.

Because Tony's wife was an elementary school teacher and could not take time to escort their daughter to doctor appointments, Tony took care of everything.

During these months, Tony's days were erratic. He lived a dual life. He had to be there for his daughter, and he had to go to work. He said he did not function well at the office. He told his supervisor of his trauma and, compassionately, the superior told him to do whatever he had to do. Although the superior took care of Tony's schedule needs, such as allowing him to use annual leave time whenever he had to care for his daughter, Tony realized his emotional needs were not being met. He had nowhere to go to talk out his feelings. He said he did not even know how to express his feelings. He said, "My heart was ripped in two and my whole body ached." As a father, he wished he could spend all his time supporting his daughter and do nothing else. But even in trying to help her, he felt powerless.

The Manager's Responsibilities

In the second session you can expect to hear differing comments about how managers should interact with TLE employees. Logically, Tony's superior was good to give him time off without making a fuss and to go easy on his work requirements, but emotionally and in empathy the superior didn't score very highly.

Second session discussions usually affirm the importance of TLE employees' personalities and the need to allow for a variety of performance expectations upon their return. All will agree that managers should give work assignments to returning TLE employees gradually, allowing the employee to familiarize slowly when returning after a trauma. Managers among the participants will also agree that understanding about introverted and extroverted personalities would help them understanding their employees, but they may point out that managers also have different personalities. "Some of us are outgoing, others are aloof and cool." So, managers need to understand themselves, too. Perhaps Tony's supervisor was an introvert and had a hard time dealing with heavy emotions in someone else. Tony, a manager himself, acknowledged that, before the Dialogue Circle, he wasn't much good at empathizing with returning TLE employees.

Managers in a Dialogue Circle group who themselves have returned to work after a traumatic experience are usually more sensitive to the needs of returning TLE employees. But there is no guarantee that this transformation will happen. Some managers may acknowledge how, "My trauma changed me. I have learned to use my wound experience to help someone else in their pain." And, "I feel free to approach a returning TLE employee and let them know I'm available." This shift didn't happen to Tony as a manager until he experienced the Dialogue Circle. As much as he wanted and needed empathy from his superior, he seemed unable to offer the same to those traumatized people he himself managed.

Most groups recognize that individuals who are returning to the workplace after having experienced a trauma ought to be acknowledged by someone in the organization, preferably their manager. This manager should ask the returning employee what her colleagues can do for her. Groups will usually advise managers to watch for cues from the employee about how to respond, and not to intrude if the person is unwilling to share their feelings at work at this time.

Knowing how to give a referral for professional care and knowing where to send TLE employees returning to the workplace after a trauma was seen by all groups as an essential skill for any manager. For some reason, Tony's superior seemed to have missed this opportunity completely. Tony was never referred for counseling. "But, then again," admitted Tony, "neither did I refer my survivors for counseling before I did the Dialogue Circle."

There's more to Tony's story.

Tony's Worst Fear Reappears

This trauma with Melody went on for a year and a half. Finally, in the early spring of 1990 Tony and his family were told that the treatment had worked and his daughter had become 95 percent free of the cancer. But they recommended Melody continue going for tests every month. Life in Tony's family slowly began to return to some sort of normalcy.

In September 1990, Tony received another phone call from Dr. Granger stating that the doctors and specialists had run two sets of test on Melody, and they confirmed that the cancer had spread to her lymph nodes and areas around her heart.

When Tony got that phone call at his office, he said he froze at his computer. He felt paralyzed. He could not focus. He checked his watch and it was close to noon. He left the office to attend lunch-hour mass at a Catholic church nearby and pray for guidance.

After the congregation left the church, he sat there in a daze for two more hours trying to compose himself and think of how he and his family would get through this ordeal. He still had to go home to tell his wife and daughter the bad news.

As he sat in the church pew, Tony said he was angry at God. He asked God, "Why me? Why us? Why my daughter? Why are we going through this again? Why are we being punished? What did we do to deserve this?" Tony wasn't sure how he would ever collect himself to be able to talk to his family.

When Tony arrived home, he called his wife and daughter together and told them about the phone call he got from Dr. Granger. They all hugged each other and cried.

The doctors did not want to perform surgery, so they immediately began the treatment again. Tony's nightmare only got worse. He had to go to Melody's school to arrange for her to be tutored and then talk to the cheerleading coach, since Melody had just made the cheerleading squad. As Tony took complete charge of Melody's care, all types of feelings were welling up inside him. He says, "I felt inadequate. I wanted to make it more comfortable for Melody and I couldn't. I felt her pain and wanted to take her place, and I couldn't."

Tony and Connie decided to join a support group for parents. This helped them to understand what other parents were going through. Many evenings after leaving the group, they found themselves being thankful they did not have to bear some of the extra complications other parents were experiencing.

Tony said his relationship with his wife at this time was also severely stressed. Being an elementary school teacher, Connie would come home and would want to talk about her classes. Tony admits that he was not interested in her work; he was totally preoccupied with his daughter's health. Because of this conflict, his wife sought a counselor. Instead of helping her stay in the marriage, the counselor suggested they separate. Connie returned home and discussed her feelings with Tony, and for the first time they talked about their relationship, their deep love for each other, and their need for mutual support. They ended up staying together and supporting each other.

At this same time, their other children were feeling the stress of Melody's new bout with illness. Tony's two sons, away at college, said they had lost interest in their schoolwork and wanted to come home to help the family through this crisis. Tony urged them to stay in school. His younger son Robert said, "I wish I had the cancer and not Melody." Melody's answer to her younger brother was, "I can handle this, but I couldn't if it was happening to you."

When employees are not good at asking for help, a manager's communication skills become important.

Communication Skills

One Dialogue Circle group that focused in their first session on the importance of communication skills about putting out a welcome mat for returning TLE employees, continued with this topic throughout the second and third sessions. In encouraging managers to develop good "listening ear" skills, they suggested the following:

- *Develop active listening skills.* These are important when dealing with an individual returning to the workplace after a trauma.
- *Be cautious* in approaching returning TLE employees and be sincere in your acknowledgment of them.
- *Show compassion.* Unfortunately, while some people naturally have compassion, others do not. Nevertheless, it is a quality that should be shown toward returning TLE employees.
- *Don't offer false compassion.* It's worse than saying nothing at all.
- *Don't try to play therapist in the workplace.* As a rule, besides showing compassion, encourage the employee to go to the EAP for counseling or at least to talk out whatever is troubling him.

A traumatized employee who has a strong religious faith may often turn to a spiritual director for guidance, consolation, and courage to deal with the emotional pain. A manager may find it helpful to suggest that such a returning employee seek support from their church community.

After months of chemotherapy and radiation treatments, Tony's daughter Melody was scheduled to go to the hospital for her first check-up. That same day, Tony went to the church and prayed. Some weeks before, he had discovered a book on the lives of the saints. He was especially attracted to the story of St. Solanus Casey, "Nothing Short of a Miracle." This saint, who had a healing ministry, died in 1957. Solanus recommended that one should be thankful first and accept the will of God before praying for healing. Tony began to pray by thanking the saint and said, "If my daughter's cancer is worsening and we could lose her, I want the strength to live with her with this disease." From that day on, Tony continued to pray with the attitude recommended by the saint.

A few days after the check-up, Dr. Granger called Tony and told him that the team of doctors had just completed two tests on Melody, and there was no sign of the cancer. He said they wanted to do another set of tests the next week. The following week, the oncologist called Tony and said the doctors from the cancer board reviewed the third set of tests, and there were clearly no signs of cancer. The doctor told Tony that Melody would require no additional treatment, since she was now completely free of cancer.

Tony, Connie, and Melody met with the team of doctors, who could not explain what had happened to bring about the young woman's health. Tony said, "A miracle has happened to our family." The doctors acknowledged they would never forget this case and could not offer a medical explanation.

Tony's World Today

Tony decided to become a deacon in the Catholic Church and now ministers to other like him who have gone through different phases of trauma. With his career back on track, his work world grew busy with assignments and travel. Family life is normal again, too. He and his wife just returned from their first trip to Italy.

By the time I met Tony, two of his sons were married, one daughter was in college, and Melody had recently become a biomedical engineer with her first job at a nationally respected clinic. She was operating the sophisticated machinery and ministering to patients who were ill and seeking assistance in their traumatic times. Although Tony and Connie miss her, they wish her well. A part of them still feels the effects of their own trauma but awe at how their life has unfolded.

During my interview with Tony before the Dialogue Circle began, I asked him how this trauma changed him and his life. He admitted that prior to it he could never talk to anyone about a terminal illness. Now, he is very comfortable in talking and ministering to the sick and dying but not so much as a manager at work.

We then focused on the workplace, and I asked him if he thought supervisors today were better able to deal with returning TLE employees than they were when Melody was first diagnosed with cancer. He said no. He said most supervisors still avoid employees after a trauma, mostly, he thought, because they do not know how to relate to them. He wished also that teams at work could help people support each other more when a trauma occurs in their lives.

From my observations of Tony in the Dialogue Circle and afterward, he was a pivotal person in the group. He willingly shared his trauma story, which helped others talk about their trauma. In group dialogue he was very forthcoming and articulate. During the second session, Tony reported that he had gone back to the office and talked more openly and freely to an employee who had just experienced a death in her family.

After the Dialogue Circle, he expressed to the group how he had benefited immensely from others in the group and felt he now knew many new ways he could be helpful as a manager to other returning TLE employees. He thanked me especially because he made a new friend in the Dialogue Circle group: a man who had left the priesthood, got married, and began working for the department. He asked him if they could have lunch.

Communication and Group Climate

I usually open each session of a Dialogue Circle by reading notes I have taken from the previous session. This creates an opportunity for group members to refresh their memories on what they discussed the last time. It also gives them a chance to improve or refine what they said then.

At the opening, I might also take the time to comment on the discussion process and re-motivate the group, saying something like: "Last session, our group interaction worked quite well. In the beginning some individuals dominated the exchange of ideas, but as the session progressed all members became active participants. The main reason for the success of this group is that you all came here to address a specific need. You wanted to help managers and coworkers with the reentry process of a TLE employee. Every one of you felt the need personally. That's why you work so well together."

When a number of people get together to discuss an issue that is important to them, their attitudes and behavior can create a defensive or supportive climate. When defensive behavior occurs, individuals perceive themselves being threatened or they anticipate a climate of threat in the group. They feel unsafe and insecure. They feel separate and alone, and they usually withdraw from participating. On the other hand, supportive behavior usually has the opposite effect. They feel safe and secure. People feel close, connected. They want to share and they want to learn from others. They find consensus in their decisions.

In her book, *Focus Like a Laser Beam: 10 Ways to Do What Matters Most*, Lisa Haneberg observed that we communicate both verbally and nonverbally and that we are open to input and use methods that produce regular and effective feedback. She also introduced a process that she calls "feed forward" on how you can improve on an idea *for the future*.[1] The process can be started by anyone who knows their task. The Dialogue Circle is precisely a "feed forward" process, as it helps participants create a better future climate in the workplace for TLE employees.

In an article titled "Effective Group Communication Processes," David Ingram explains how a group's overall effectiveness hinges to a great extent on the effectiveness of the participants' communication abilities. Without positive flows of communication, misunderstandings can occur between groups, creating a fractious work environment.[2] Ingram's insight shows how important the facilitator's role is in a Dialogue Circle in creating openness in communication.

First, regarding *openness* in a Dialogue Circle, supportive participants show a definite interest in the perception of others and listen to their points of view. Honesty and respect are important aspects in a Dialogue Circle. They are lending a listening ear. They also tend to be open-minded. They are willing to risk and generously share their trauma stories. This usually creates a positive climate for trust.

I recall one employee who shared his trauma story and in talking, gave insight to what he was feeling about his work, his supervisor, and the organization. Others probed further by asking him questions. Elaborating on his own trauma—his teenage son had committed suicide—he continued to take the risk in sharing his insights about what went on inside him emotionally after the event, which helped create trust among participants and allowed members to bond with each other. This bond continued outside the Dialogue Circle. After the second session, some of the members attended a retirement party for a colleague in their department. I noticed some of these participants, previously unacquainted, talking with each other and sharing work experiences at this party.

In their openness in telling their trauma story to the group, they gave insights to each other. For example, one young woman who had been raped said when she returned to the workplace after her trauma, she "was there, and not there." She told, for example, how she might be sitting in a staff meeting but her mind and all her attention was back at the scene of the trauma. She explained further that returning TLE employees like her were often "not the same person" when they returned to the workplace, and she described how she saw herself differently since the trauma. She acknowledged that she sometimes feels as if she was a dirty and shameful person, even though she knows in her head that these feelings shouldn't be there.

Second, *trust* in a group setting comes gradually, no matter how supportive participants may be. Trust is built in small increments. For example, in the second session when Tony shared the trauma story of his daughter's cancer, it had a rippling effect of trust within the group. Soon, another manager talked about her son's murder. Each story created another manager layer of "safe trust" in the group. Soon after that, another manager from the Office of Public Policy shared his trauma. This manager told the group that his son has been in a coma three years because of an automobile accident. Even today, the son is unable to recognize anyone and cannot even squeeze his father's hand. This man asked the group how they could help him deal with his ongoing trauma, because it is with him every day. He shared with the group how, in the early months of the trauma, everyone was attentive to him and his needs, but as time went on few people asked about his son. Nowadays at work almost no one ever brings up the topic. The group surged in support of this manager who carried such an emotional burden to work with him every day. But such a story comes out only when the group has built up enough mutual trust to sustain powerful feelings.

The third quality a supportive group builds is *empathy*. Empathy is also a quality that just about every Dialogue Circle group says is needed in managers for dealing with returning TLE employees. Groups discuss this quality at length, with managers usually admitting not knowing how to show empathy and asking "What is it?"

Experts suggest that empathy means learning to understand the values, meaning, and symbols of another person. Others describe empathy as "walking in another person's moccasins" or feeling what another person feels. In groups I facilitated, many managers were not sure how much empathy they should show the returning TLE employees. But they did realize that productivity in returning TLE employees would be lower if managers did not deal positively with employees and their trauma.

I recall one employee who shared in the group his frustration and anger about his supervisor. He told the group members that his son had suffered a head injury and he had to be out of work a month to care for his son. When he returned, his boss never asked about his son. "It's been five years," he said, "and to this date, he has never approached me about the matter." By sharing their trauma stories and their treatment at the hands of unfeeling managers, returning TLE employees give managers a "new lens" to see how an employee actually feels when returning to the workplace and how they view a thoughtless manager.

As I observed Tony in the interview and Dialogue Circle, I recognized a man who was eager to share his experiences with someone. As part of the interactive dynamics of the Dialogue Circle, he was the first person to tell his trauma story. He not only set the tone for other people to talk openly during the second session, he took the biggest risk. He talked about men and their feelings, and "how I struggled every day because no one was available in the workplace to comfort me." Individuals in the group were visibly moved by his story and, as a consequence, others were willing to share their own trauma experiences.

A Disruptive TLE Employee

Sometimes, if a Dialogue Circle group focuses on the issue of "problem employee" during their first session, the same theme will naturally arise in the second session. They may talk about the manager's dilemma and what to do when returning employees either refuse to do their assignments or do the opposite of what they are asked to do.

In one group, they brought up a special kind of problem employee: What does a manager do when the employee not only recounts the trauma story but talks incessantly about it?

One female manager who experienced the loss of her son suggested, "Allow the TLE employee space to discuss the trauma. Don't push them to talk, but don't let their retelling their story become disruptive in the office."

After much discussion, the group suggested the following guidelines for dealing with TLE employees who tend to talk incessantly about their traumatic experience:

- If TLE employees' talking incessantly is consuming their coworker's time, the manager *must* intercede. One suggestion was for the manager to recommend that the TLE employee see someone in the EAP for counseling.
- Try to refocus the talking employees' interest on the task that needs to be accomplished, then in a gentle way, with some diplomacy, try to get them back on the work track.
- Give the returning TLE employees alternate work options where there is less temptation to keep talking. Help everyone in the group to understand that there are different types of trauma and the recovery process may be longer for a specific type of trauma or for certain personalities.
- When the TLE employees first return to the workplace, it is important how and when the manager approaches. An early meeting will usually reveal the employees' special needs and perhaps relieve their need to keep retelling the trauma story and share their experience with the manager.

Summary

As I continue to facilitate Dialogue Circles on trauma and recovery in the workplace, I am continually impressed by the power of this interactive learning model in bringing individuals together to discuss a sensitive topic about which they all have strong feelings. Tony, in particular, said he had learned new concepts and new approaches while listening to some of the others' responses. He also stated that he learned a lot when managers and employees were trying to come to agreement about the conflict between "empathy and productivity." "During those discussions," he said. "I gained a new perspective about the manager's point of view."

Specifically, Tony recognized through the sharing of another participant, who happened to be a manager, the crucial importance of knowing how to deal with a "volatile employee" since such behavior could seriously affect coworkers in the workplace. When other employees and managers began asking questions on how this situation could be handled, they learned the steps that an individual manager took and the way he talked with the employee. Tony took the initiative to ask the group if guidelines could be set up for managers and employees as a kind of reference tool. He felt this would be helpful.

By the end of the Dialogue Circle's second session, participants have become a powerful interactive learning team. During the third session they learn to *offer a helping hand* and realize the importance of making the returning TLE employees feel like an integral part of the workplace team once again.

Notes

1. Lisa Haneberg, *Focus Like a Laser Beam: 10 Ways to Do What Matters Most* (San Francisco: Jossey-Bass, 2006), 89.

2. David Ingram, "Effective Group Communication Processes," 2016, smallbusiness.chron.com/effective-group-communication-processes-3187.html.

CHAPTER TWELVE

~

Offering a Helping Hand

The Third Dialogue Circle

On the Outside, On the Inside

I like to call the third stage in understanding the emotional recovery process of the returning TLE employee *offering a helping hand*. Its purpose is to invite the manager and coworkers to take the initiative in restoring their personal and professional connections with the survivor.

On their first days back to work, despite how "normal" TLE survivors may appear on the outside, they often feel disorganized, disoriented, and disconnected on the inside. Because of the traumatic event, their sense of trust in others may have been severely weakened, their sense of control over things severely shaken, their confidence toward others in the workplace unsure. For some, their life meaning is falling apart and many question their fundamental beliefs.

As a rule, coworkers are puzzled at the unusual behavior and attitude of returning TLE employees and, as a result, may show very little support toward the survivor. For various reasons, connections have been broken. The traumatic event itself has done this. A woman who has been raped or a father whose teenage son committed suicide, in their shame and embarrassment or feelings of guilt, may imagine themselves as a dirtied person or a failure as a parent, and so may presume that their coworkers see them in the same way. They may think, "My coworkers won't want to relate to me anymore."

On their part, coworkers as a rule do not know how to treat survivors. Many fellow employees expect them to have gone for counseling and have gotten "straightened out" before returning to the job. Just as returning TLE employees themselves have difficulty reconnecting with the organization, coworkers are not sure what to do, how to relate to them or suggest where they can go for assistance, if they seem to need it. This is where learning to *offer a helping hand* comes in.

Some reconnection-related questions the Dialogue Circle's third session handout ask participants to think about are:

- Can you describe some of the kinds of "connections" that typically exist between manager and employee and between worker and coworkers?
- How do people in the workplace reestablish such connections after they have been broken?
- What kinds of questions might you ask the returning TLE employees to help reestablish connections?

The Third Session

I often ask participants to rank the three Dialogue Circles sessions they attended in their order of importance. Consistently, they say that the third session—offering a helping hand to help the returning TLE employees get reconnected to the workplace community—was the most important. They recognize finally that reconnection is perhaps the most crucial stage in the reentry process.

Personally, I found this final session also to be the most challenging and the most practical for participants, since reconnecting necessarily involves all of the returning employee's coworkers. The same is true even when the returning person is a manager, like Tony, whose story we reviewed in the previous chapter.

In the third session, manager-participants tend to focus on how to discuss the trauma with coworkers and what tone to set in the organization when TLE employees return to the workplace. I recall one male manager who said, "Managers must send out the right signals to the staff." Another added, "We should include the returning trauma survivors in staff meetings, and reassure them that their status has not changed because of the trauma."

Maslow's Levels of Needs

In Maslow's pyramids of human needs, right after the need for safety and security, comes the *need to belong*. Belongingness, to be part of some human group, is essential to being alive. We all meet this essential need of belongingness in many different ways: by having a last name, being members of a certain family, having a home where we live, and using a room in that house that belongs to us. Each of these things gives us a sense of belonging, of being connected. To further develop this sense of belonging, we connect with others in neighborhoods, extended families, ethnic groups, and nations. Isn't the need to belong the reason we frame photographs of family members and display them, to remind us of our connections and the different ways we belong to each other?

Frequently, too, we bond with people in our workplace to fulfill this need of belonging. We identify ourselves as working for "this" company. We have our own office that tells the world we belong here. We have personal and financial records and other forms of connection to this organization in the manager's personnel files. We have colleagues, who call us friends and whom we look forward to seeing each day. We also like to say that we belong to a team of productive people doing something to serve society. Work does much more than help us take care of physical needs and safety and security needs. For most of us, it is a place where we, to some degree, shape our identity and our values as well as our contacts and our friendships. The workplace is a place where we often feel most ourselves.

For many, the bonds they form at work are among the strongest connections they have. For these, the workplace is, above all, the place where they feel most connected to others. And when these connections are broken, their reestablishment is a strongly felt need. As such, reestablishing connections is an important stage in the process of emotional recovery from trauma. Full emotional recovery from traumatic events is often impossible without restoring a human and personal connection to the people at work.

I did not bring up Maslow in the previous chapter because telling the trauma story has implications in at least two or three levels of human needs. Feeling ready to tell my trauma story experience to a manager or coworker means that I feel that the workplace has provided an adequate "welcome mat" for me. Do I find people ready to lend a listening ear, since telling my story to someone in the workplace is my first test of the welcome mat? If I feel free to tell my trauma story to my manager or a coworker, this tells me that my safety and security needs are in place.

Telling my story is also a test of the need to belong. When I tell my story, will it be listened to with compassion and concern, as I hope it will be? Do my coworkers accept me as a person who has been through a TLE? Do they accept me as one of them again? Do they make me feel that I belong?

Maslow identified a fourth level of need we all feel, beyond belongingness and acceptance. It is the need to be approved, to be valued, to be esteemed. It is an old saying that a family has to take in even their worst member because he lives there and belongs there. But it is one thing to live in the house where you belong, and another thing to be loved, valued, and esteemed there. The same is true in the workplace. The unspoken question in the back of the returning employee's mind is: "They may have to give me my job back, but will they still like me and value me?" Because of this esteem issue, returning TLE employees often at first will talk about only the surface level of their traumatic experience. This is how they test for safety and belongingness. When they begin telling the deeper details—the angry, shameful, anxious emotions and wishes that are roiling around inside them—they are testing for more than a sense of belonging. They are checking for your approval of them. "Do they disapprove of me or think of me as shameful or a failure? Or do they think I'm really a good person or a good parent and that I did the best I could in the circumstances?"

The important point to remember is that returning TLE employees have many basic needs to test for and, if necessary, reestablish. So, there is much more going on inside such a person than one might think. There are many questions they seek answers to, and those answers can come only from the survivor's manager and coworkers, especially those whose opinions the survivors most value.

Different Kinds of Trauma

In the third Dialogue Circle session, most groups focus on the different types of TLEs that happen. In these groups, dialogue usually continues to flow freely. Managers want to make each other aware of how these different types of TLEs complicate matters, and they ask for feedback on how to define them and deal with them.

For example, they might ask whether the death of a child or spouse would be more traumatic than witnessing an accident or the loss of one's career? Or they might ask what kinds of traumas take longest to heal? Would a person who had been raped take longer to recover than a person who was shot at in a car during a drive-by shooting? Or which traumatic events tend to change the survivor's personality? Would the survivor of a robbery, mugging, and a beating be more likely to have a changed personality than someone who had a major heart attack? Questions like these were usually directed at participants who had experienced different types of traumas.

These questions are extremely important, and they tend to rise most often during the third Dialogue Circle session, because the issue of making an emotional reconnection to the returning TLE employees depend on their answers. The story of Dede underlines the importance of this issue.

Dede's Story

Dede walked into my office for her Pre–Dialogue Circle interview. She was a petite and pretty thirty-year-old brunette with a sweet smile. By my guess, she was most men's image of the girl next door. Nothing in her appearance hinted at the horrible traumas this woman had experienced. Almost fifteen years ago, she had come to Washington, DC, from a small Midwestern town, like thousands of other women, eager to start a career in the big city. Within a year after her arrival in the Nation's Capital she had married, but got divorced before their first anniversary. The divorce papers stated "incompatibility" as the reason for the divorce, but the real reason was her husband physically and psychologically abused her. That was traumatic experience number one.

Three years later, she was raped at night outside her apartment. That day, her boss had asked her to work late and it was dark when she got off the bus for the two-block walk to her front door. She never made it home. That was trauma number two.

She was a spunky person and decided that she would never let herself be raped again, so she began working out during lunch hours at a nearby gym. If she was ever attacked again, she had told herself, she would go down fighting. By now, her interest in men had soured, she said, and she decided she would never marry again. I asked her why. She then related the real story.

Two years ago, ten years after her rape, she was in a restaurant with some other women from the office staff having dinner and enjoying girl talk on a winter's evening. She hadn't been feeling too well all week and told her companions she was going home, since it looked like they'd be chatting there for hours.

As she left the restaurant alone for her car, a tall man from the bar followed her out to the parking lot and began to attack her. I'm sure he expected no resistance from the petite Dede, but she fought back with all the strength she had built up working out in the gym. Nevertheless, her attacker beat and bruised her pretty badly. He hit her ankle somehow in a way that fractured it. At this point, another woman happened to be driving by and, seeing what was going on, began beeping her car horn. However, she did not stop her car or get out. But the man was enough distracted by the honking and headlights for Dede to get into her car and lock the door. She drove out of the parking lot as quickly as she could.

For half an hour she drove randomly through the streets, suspecting that her attacker may have gotten into his car and was following her. In case he was tracking her, she did not want him to know where she lived, so she parked about three blocks from her apartment and ran most of the way home. "My foot felt as though it had fallen off," she said. "I don't know how I managed to run on my fractured ankle. I was screaming with the pain of it. My body must have been pumping adrenaline like crazy for me not to have collapsed in pain on the sidewalk."

"The next morning," she explained, "I awoke all bruised and my ankle was swollen and throbbing. Unfortunately, I decided to telephone the police and tell them what had happened in the restaurant parking lot the night before, and ask for a ride to the hospital to take care of my ankle. Instead of compassion, I got abuse. Their interrogation of me was one more traumatic experience. They asked me questions like 'Were you provocatively dressed in the restaurant? Were you giving the man come-on signals? Did he follow you to your car because you asked him to? Besides,' they said, 'if this guy was as big as you claimed he was, there is no way you could have fended him off. And, according to the doctors who took x-rays of your ankle, they said there is no way in the world you could have walked, let alone run, three blocks to your apartment.'"

"They didn't believe a word I said," she told me. "They were convinced I was lying." To make matters worse, the police called in a psychiatrist who examined me and decided, like the police, that I was lying and needed to be committed to the psychiatric ward of the hospital. I was in the hospital anyway with my fractured ankle, which was now broken, probably because I ran for three blocks on it. But I was humiliated to be treated as an insane person."

"I telephoned my family in Ohio," she went on, "and two of my brothers came to visit me. I expected that they at least would express some sympathy for me, but in questioning me about the incident, they were as bad as the police. They wanted to know if I had been the instigator of the attempted rape. They asked how I had dressed, how I had behaved in the restaurant, and was I in the habit of getting guys to come on to me. These were my own brothers! They were accusing me of being a seductress and implying I had gotten the beating that I deserved."

When I suggested that her brothers' visit was itself another traumatic experience for her, about her fourth or fifth in a few days, she agreed.

"But that wasn't all," she continued. "I had been working in an office for over a year and had been very well liked for my work and productivity. When Sid, my manager, came to see me in the hospital, he started off by saying he was sorry I was not well. I expected at least he would offer some sympathy for what I had been through. He knew me well enough to know that I wasn't crazy or used to making up stories. But a moment later he told me that I was fired. When I began to object, he held up his hand, as if to tell me there was nothing to say. 'Look Dede,' he said going out the door, 'it's so much easier to replace you than to wait for you to get better. Don't bother to come back to the shop. I'll have your check mailed to your apartment.'"

Dede is no longer working with that firm. When she finally recovered from her broken ankle and the police had stopped harassing her, she started her life over in a new job with the federal government, where she has been working for almost two years.

I asked her if anyone in her new job knew about her traumatic experiences. She said no. I asked if she would be willing to talk about any of those experiences in the Dialogue Circle.

She wasn't sure. She would "test the waters. Maybe in the second or third session, if I get up enough courage to create a dialogue with the participants, I will tell my story."

I assured her she was free to share her story in any way she wanted, completely or partially. "Any one of your traumatic life experiences would be enough to challenge the group," I told her. "Your whole story might even overwhelm them, as it has me."

Dede Tells Her Story

Dede did decide to tell most of her story in the third session. After she finished, the group was quiet for a few moments. During the past two sessions, they had developed strong feelings of compassion for one another. Hearing that she had been dismissed from her job without a thought infuriated them. They expressed anger at the callousness of the police officers who had questioned her, at the psychiatrist who had her committed, at her brothers for blaming her for the mugging. It took a few minutes for the group to cool down.

To bring the group back to the third session's theme of reconnecting, I posed a hypothetical question to the group.

"We know that in fact Dede's boss Sid was a scoundrel and couldn't be bothered with keeping her job waiting for her," I began. "But let's imagine he was a good guy. Let's imagine on that first visit to the hospital to see her he created a basic welcome mat, assuring Dede that her job was secure and that the rest of the staff were asking for her and wanted to come visit her. Let's further suppose that when he visited her in the hospital a second time, he let Dede tell her story and he listened empathetically. But now, six weeks have gone by and it is time for Dede, the TLE employee, to return to the workplace. What kinds of issues would it have posed for Sid and her coworkers to reconnect with Dede? Let's start by listing the different issues that will affect reconnecting with Dede."

Within a few moments the group had identified several factors that would influence the reconnecting task facing Sid and Dede's coworkers.

- prior relationships
- the gender issue
- returning too soon
- personality changes in the survivor

We discussed each of these four issues in turn, in general, and, specifically, for Dede's situation.

1. Prior Relationships

The success of people in the office reconnecting with returning TLE employees depends on the relationship the employees had with their coworkers prior to the trauma. Most participants agreed that the ease of reconnection would depend on these prior relationships. If relationships had been good before the trauma, then the returning TLE employee's transition might be easier. And if prior relationships had been poor, strained or nonexistent, the transition might be uphill all the way.

When we considered Dede's manager Sid as he really felt toward her, we decided it was most likely a nonexistent relationship. Sid saw her as an object, as a replaceable part of his office machinery. To him, she wasn't even a human being who deserved respect, care, and protection in her situation. They did not see much hope for reconnection, since there had been no connection in the first place. Dede concurred in their analysis. She felt as her fellow participants did.

When we considered an imaginary Sid as I had described him—compassionate, caring, thoughtful—it was a completely different story. The group agreed that reconnection in the workplace would be much easier. In fact, they pointed out that by his coming to the hospital and listening to her trauma story, he had already created a *welcome mat*, provided a *listening ear*, and offered a *helping hand*. In such a powerful gesture, he had kept the connection with her. It had never broken.

Dede kept silent through this, but wore a wry smile. It was easier for the rest of the group to reimagine the story in a positive way than for Dede, since the image of the real Sid was inerasable in her mind.

Dede's coworkers, we decided, with Dede's agreement, would have an easier time reconnecting to her than Sid. But, when someone in the group asked Dede whether any of her friends who were at the restaurant with her had phoned or visited, she replied, "Very few, and never more than once."

Participants wondered why this was so. "Were your coworkers embarrassed?" they asked. "Were they frightened? Did Sid tell them to avoid you? Did Sid make up some story to keep them away? Were they afraid that if they befriended you or talked positively about you at work, Sid would fire them too?"

Dede, of course, did not know the answers to their questions.

Then the group began asking themselves, if they were Dede's coworkers, would they have the courage to remain her friend and confront Sid about his cold indifference in firing her. This question hanging in the air was followed by some soul searching.

When I asked the group to explore more broadly the prior relationship theme, one person brought up the flip side of the issue. "It takes two to make a relationship," he said. "What if the manager is a nice guy and the employee surviving the trauma has been a perennial pest? How do managers and coworkers honestly reconnect to someone they'd rather not be connected to?"

One manager added that coworkers of a perennial pest can get stressed out by such a returning TLE employees, especially if the survivor previously exhibited violent behavior in the workplace or had verbally threatened individuals. He stressed that this was a serious problem that he personally had to deal with. "When complaints come to me from this guy's coworkers," he explained, "I have to deal with the problem. I can't shirk these responsibilities."

As a facilitator, I put his question to the group, I said, "Suppose the returning TLE employee had been a problem employee, a borderline performer, or did not always do his/her work?"

"This could create special reconnection challenges for the manager and coworkers," acknowledged one participant, "But it may also be a wonderful opportunity to establish new and more productive relationships with the problem person."

I encouraged the respondent to develop her thought.

"Perhaps," she said, "before the traumatic event it was common for managers and coworkers alike to treat this problem person with coldness, annoyance or even outright exclusion from the rest of the staff. Providing a welcome mat in the workplace for such a person and lending a listening ear to listen to them tell their trauma story creates a very different atmosphere from what the returning employee might expect. And in this caring atmosphere the person might be ready and willing to change his behavior."

Someone else agreed with her point. "With returning problem workers, people in the office do not want to reestablish the prior strained relationships," he said, "We'd rather initiate a new kind of relationship."

"But," interrupted a participant who had usually been quiet, "for many of us who have been treated badly by such a person—and I have!—it may be quite difficult to let bygones be bygones."

"But if we don't do it," came the reply, "we can only expect to have problems with this returning TLE employee worse than they were before."

Most groups recognize that, no matter what problems a person may have had as a worker prior to their traumatic life experience, when that person returns after a trauma, that person is different because of his experience in the emotional recovery process. That person is in need of special efforts and understanding from managers and coworkers. Managers must realize that a traumatized employee is a changed person. Even though the TLE person may look the same, talk the same, and even dress the same, an inner transformation has happened. And it needs to be recognized and acknowledged by everyone in the office.

One manager, speaking from personal experience, said that the returning employee should be greeted and his absence should be acknowledged. Another manager suggested, "The day a TLE employee returned to the workplace would be an excellent time for a dialogue, in essence, as part of welcoming the employee back to the work environment and helping them feel once again part of a team."

Another manager said she found it very helpful to send emails periodically to TLE employees who were still at home, before they returned to work. She stated that human contact was a priority in cases like these and managers needed to know and understand that priority, and to take time to do their part.

2. Returning Too Soon

The next issue we discussed regarding the connection theme was returning to the workplace too soon after a traumatic life experience. Time is an important factor in the emotional recovery from trauma. Although groups usually ask how long it takes for the returning TLE employee to heal from a trauma, they quickly acknowledge from experience that no one can give an exact estimate of the weeks or months it will take to get over a TLE—if ever. We all have hopes and expectations in this regard, but usually they are way off the mark.

Dede said it was two years since her traumatic episodes with the mugger, the police, the psychiatrist, her brother, and Sid. "I would like to think that

I have recovered from it. I've been seeing a psychologist every week for well over a year, trying to work through the bitterness toward it all. I probably wouldn't have started looking for a job as early as I did, but I was running out of money. Nobody stopped sending me bills just because I'd had a trauma."

"Is that when you started working for the new agency?" I asked.

"Yes," she replied. "And my bosses here have been great. So are my friends in the office. My manager here is everything Sid wasn't."

It would be an ideal world if all managers were compassionate, closely monitored the traumatized employee's treatment and the emotional recovery process, and had the power to play a key role in deciding when an employee returns to the workplace after their trauma. But organizational policies and health insurance companies usually have a much stronger voice in this matter.

One manager in the group felt traumatized employees are encouraged to return to the workplace far too soon, well before they are ready to work. "As managers," he said to the group, "we must be sensitive to this too-early-return policy in receiving in the employee back to the organization. We're the ones who have to deal with it because we're the ones responsible for the returning person's work assignments."

A female manager who herself had been a traumatized person returning to the workplace—her mother had died suddenly—stated that when she returned after her trauma, her supervisor did not hurry her reconnection, and gave her a choice of assignments. "He handed me a paper with a list of activities and meeting schedules," she said, "and told me that when I was ready I could choose to be involved in any or all of these activities. I did go to some of those meetings and though I was present physically I was not there mentally." She said this freedom given by her manager helped her tremendously because she did not feel pressured to perform. "He let me monitor my own emotional state and create my own time frame for getting re-involved in the organization."

Managers especially emphasize that the reconnection process is a lot more difficult than it seems. "The office may be going at a frantic pace, but when an employee is returning after a trauma," explained one manager, "you need to shut out all that is going on in the office, stop completely at least for a few minutes, and be totally focused on the returning employee. And in these first moments of reconnection, you need to be sensitive and creative because every returning employee is different and has different needs. There is no formula that I know of that will work for every returning traumatized employee."

In that same group, another manager added a caveat. "I don't disagree with you," he said, "but I find that a lot of managers tend to over-protect the returning TLE employee, rather than create opportunities for more open dialogue between the survivor and their coworkers. I'm for alerting other staff members in the group when a traumatized person is returning to the workplace and encouraging them to help put out a welcome mat and lend an ear to listen to their stories as well as me. Yes, reconnecting with me, the manager, may be important to the returning employee, but reestablishing connection to each member of the staff is at least as important because the returning person will be spending a lot more time with them than with me."

Near the end of a third session, a manager in a different group said he had a personal situation that was rather unique and asked the group's help. His trauma was ongoing, he explained. His son had been in a car accident and was presently in a semi-comatose state. He visits his son daily and his condition has not changed. This situation has gone on for three years. His supervisors were very helpful in the beginning, but now they do not ask any questions or show any concern for his situation, and it's business as usual. He said he would welcome some concerned inquiry from his colleagues. He asked me and the group to consider his situation and think about what he could do. As it was the end of the session, the most the group could offer was its sympathy and compassion. But this manager's problem points to another area of trauma research beyond the scope of my work, the chronic trauma, in contrast to the single TLE that has been the focus of this book.

3. The Gender Issue

One important issue that is often discussed during the third session is the different ways gender might affect coping with trauma. In Dede's group discussing this issue, I asked whether, in their experience, women or men cope better after a trauma when coming back to the workplace.

One employee felt that men did not like to talk about very personal matters in the office, and that they might be more open about such matters outside the workplace. She said that after her sudden-divorce trauma, the men in her carpool showed empathy toward her and talked about some of their own emotional struggles, but *only* in the car. "Once they stepped into the office," she said, "it was all business and they never brought up their personal matters. As soon as we stepped into the office, it was as though they had shifted personalities. At least it was true of the three men in our carpool."

A female manager whose son was killed concurred with her. "My husband keeps his feelings inside. I went to a therapist, who helped me," she said. "But my husband still has not dealt with the death of our son. He's still holding it all inside, and I'm waiting for it to blow." Some men in the group suggested that men tend to internalize their feelings and find other ways to work them out, even though they do not want to talk about their traumas.

Another employee whose daughter had been diagnosed with cancer said his wife went into group therapy but he wouldn't go. However, he agreed to attend with her a cancer group for parents. When someone in the group asked why he went to one but not the other, he made a distinction between the purpose of the two groups. He saw the cancer group offering guidance, and the therapy group offering support. He said, "Men want guidance, not support. I guess women want both."

4. Personality Changes in the Survivor

During the second session, the issue of personality types is often brought up because it affects how willing a returning TLE employee may be to tell their trauma story or experience to a manager or coworkers. Extroverted types often like to process their feelings aloud, so it is more likely that an outgoing person may feel more like talking about a traumatic incident than an introverted one, who prefers usually to process feelings internally. The same emphasis might hold true for a survivor making reconnections with others in the office.

But the issue that frequently arises in the third session is about internal changes that have happened in the survivor of the traumatic experience. When we asked Dede about this, she said she could only speak for herself, but she certainly had changed. "Actually," she said. "I've changed at least twice during the two years since I was attacked. After the mugging and all the rest that followed, I began doubting myself. Can all of these people really be wrong, I wondered? Is it possible that I am really a lewd person? Do I unconsciously send sexual messages to men? Should I share the guilt in the mugging? Was I somehow asking for it? So, at first I really lost faith in myself and in my judgment. I wondered if I should feel ashamed and guilty. That was my first personality change. I went from a lot of self-confidence and pride in my accomplishments to being full of doubts. It would have been terrible if I tried to come back to work at the old place then. Fortunately, I began seeing a great therapist who helped me to put things in perspective. I had done as well as I could in my own self-defense and self-care. In fact, I realized that I had been courageous and brave through it all. With this perspective, I was able to slowly rebuild a strong self-image. Only then was I truly ready to come back to work—even though I had already worked in the new office for a number of months. Luckily, I was not expected to tell my trauma story at the new place, because nobody there knew anything about it—or me."

Summary

After facilitating a number of Dialogue Circles on trauma and emotional recovery, I am more convinced than ever of the power of this interactive learning format in educating people in the workplace. Managers and coworkers do not have to become psychologists or counselors to be able to aid a returning TLE employee in the emotional recovery process. They can be tremendously helpful with just a little bit of education.

The transformative results of the Dialogue Circle are evident in participants on the three levels. They are changed (1) cognitively, (2) attitudinally, and (3) behaviorally. In other words, after the Dialogue Circle, they (1) think differently about and how long it takes to recover emotionally from a traumatic event, (2) have developed different attitudes toward returning TLE employees, and (3) behave differently toward them. Let's look at each.

Cognitively, when participants have finished the three sessions of the Dialogue Circle, they are able among other things, to identify TLEs and distinguish a single-event trauma from a chronic traumatic situation. They can define the three stages of emotional recovery and describe with examples of what a person goes through in each stage. They can identify different levels of basic human needs related to trauma. They can define terms like empathy, emotional welcome mat, active listening, and reconnections. They recognize the influence of trauma on different personality types.

Attitudinally, they are cognizant of the need for patience and timing in dealing with traumatized people. They acknowledge the importance of compassion and empathy, of developing listening skills, and of letting the survivor take the lead. Employees learn about the manager's perspective in relating to returning TLE employees, while managers learn about the coworkers' perspective. Managers hear what other managers have done or not done. Employees who have gone through the returning process tell what they wish their managers had done. An important issue that one participant may forget, another remembers. Together they sift out what approaches they think are helpful and which are not. All this happens in stimulating dialogue in a spirit of openness to learning. Everyone's attitudes are changed.

Behaviorally, listening to each other's experiences they develop easy, simple, and direct ways to treat the returning TLE employee. In helping support the person's emotional recovery from trauma, they learn some easy ways to *put out a welcome mat* in the workplace, practice skills for *lending a listening ear* to evoke the trauma story, and accumulate practical hints for *offering a helping hand* to reestablish connections with the returning employee. Everyone feels the wonderful energy in the group for wanting to be helpful, for wanting the process to work.

I feel more convinced than ever that the Dialogue Circle can effectively fill an important missing step in the organization's treatment of the returning TLE employee.

PART III

~

SOME SPECIAL CIRCUMSTANCES

CHAPTER THIRTEEN

~

When an Entire Group
Is Traumatized, How Do
Managers and Employees Cope?

When a Group Is Traumatized

Throughout this book, I have focused on the individual worker returning to work after a personal TLE. But, what if an entire office staff is traumatized by the same experience? Such a precipitating event might be an office break-in, a deranged and disgruntled former employee on a shooting spree in the office, a secret terrorist incident with biological agents that can produce sickness and death among the staff, a fire or explosion in the building, threatening letters sent to the office, and so on.

If everyone in the office is traumatized by an event, who is there to provide a welcome mat for everyone, to listen to their stories, to reconnect them to each other and to the workplace? This is a different situation from the case of an individual TLE employee returning to the workplace. But such situations happen. They can happen in a business office, government building, post office, school, church, or synagogue.

A Group Traumatic Experience

Charlie was the type of worker who joked with everyone and made the office a fun place to work. He cut out cartoons and left them on his colleagues' office chairs and gave them funny surprise gifts. It was only natural for him, as he did one afternoon, to volunteer to work late to finish a budget project that was due the following morning. Joanne, his coworker who had edited the draft report, agreed to stay with him to finish the final copy.

As everyone was leaving for the day, Charlie and Joanne decided to take a break and go for a bite to eat before doing the final copy. The Grub'n'Pub was just down the street, where office staff typically met for happy hour, going-away parties, and holiday toasts. This particular evening, Charlie was feeling pretty good. When he and Joanne walked in, Benny the owner of the Grub'n'Pub led them to a special table. As the piano was playing, Joanne started to sing and turned to Charlie to get his reaction. The first time she turned, he was busy talking to some other people. A few minutes passed and she turned toward him again, still singing. This time Charlie's face was resting on the table. Joanne thought nothing of it, since Charlie always liked playing jokes. When the song ended, she called his name but he did not respond. When Joanne looked more closely, he still was slumped over. When she touched him, he fell to the floor. She screamed! Luckily, a doctor was in the pub at the time. They called an ambulance and they rushed Charlie to the hospital. When the ambulance arrived at the hospital, Charlie was pronounced dead.

The following morning, unaware of Charlie's death, everyone in the office was preparing for a staff meeting. It was business as usual. Everyone was ready to hear the budget briefing that Charlie and Joanne had prepared. But neither Charlie nor Joanne was present. Suddenly, the secretary screamed and the director came running over to her. He took the phone from her. It was Charlie's wife on the other end. She told him that Charlie died of a heart attack the previous evening. Joanne had left a message on the director's phone mail about Charlie's death, but he had not picked it up.

Unprepared Staff

The sudden death of a coworker in an office is a traumatic event for the employees. Shock is what the employees in Charlie's group had experienced upon hearing the news. Shock is a physical and psychological trauma that lasts much longer than most people realize. It affects a person's normal mental functioning. People in shock see and hear things, but the words and images often do not register. It is during this phase that people need the greatest support.

Trying to understand the sheer belief that such an event actually happened would require some attention to a process called "wound-healing." Dr. Jamie Marich, in her book *Trauma Made Simple: Competencies in Assessment, Treatment and Working with Survivors*, explains the process. She states, "Healing needs to occur from the inside out, [it is] a process that can take a great deal of time. This process is the middle stage. After a wound heals, it generally leaves a scar. In cases of relatively benign wounding, that scar may clear up altogether. With more significant injuries, a person may need to get used to living with a scar or whatever aftermath is left behind after the wound heals."[1]

No workplace is truly prepared to deal with the sudden death of a co-worker. A workmate and friend had died. Someone with whom you have been accustomed to sit near and share thoughts with day after day has suddenly disappeared. You used to spend eight hours a day chatting, joking, planning, negotiating with him. This daily intimate communication is stopped in its tracks. In many ways, a close-knit work environment is like a family—they have feelings for each other. They bond with each other just as siblings do. They, too, share a closeness that is sometimes hard to define. The employees that worked with Charlie were grief-stricken, immobilized, and numb. They tried to seek consolation from each other but a vacuum had been created in the office. Charlie was no longer around to joke with his colleagues.

In his book *The Body Keeps the Score: Brain, Mind and Body in the Healing of Trauma*, Dr. Bessel van der Kolk states the following: "Trauma robs you of the feeling that you are in charge of yourself, of what I call self-leadership— the challenge of recovery to re-establish ownership of your body and your mind—of yourself. This involves (1) finding a way to become calm and focused, (2) learning to maintain that calm in response to images, thoughts, sounds, or physical sensations that remind you of the past, (3) finding a way to be fully alive in the present and engage with people around you, (4) not having to keep secrets from yourself, including secrets about the ways that you have managed to survive."[2]

There are always important steps to follow, social rituals to prepare for and carry out. First came preparing for the funeral. Mr. Carter, the staff director, called Charlie's wife and, when asked, said he would be honored to give the eulogy. Later that day, he visited with each employee to talk about Charlie and learn how he had interacted with them. At the funeral, the tribute to Charlie was not only moving but also revelatory. Charlie's congregation and family learned things about him and his work relationships that they had never known. Mr. Carter said, "Charlie was more than part of the social fabric of the office. He also was an excellent employee who cared about people." The eulogy emphasized how Charlie's coworkers grew to love and see him as part of their work family and how they would miss him as people miss close friends. Charlie's wife was appreciative of their sensitivity, and asked Mr. Carter for a copy of his prepared words.

After the funeral came readjusting to workplace life without Charlie. Coming back to work, the staff faced an uncertain terrain no one knew how to navigate. Although the traumatic event had ended, the staff's reaction did not. According to George A. Bonanno in his book, *The Other Side of Sadness: What the New Science of Bereavement Tells Us about Life after Loss*, "Some people suffer from 'prolonged grief.'"[3] That is what happened to Mr. Carter's office staff. Individual employees were overwhelmed with sadness and could not work. Everyone found it difficult to adjust back to the workplace. When the staff got back to the office, for example, Joanne was unable to concentrate. Her imagination refused to stop reliving Charlie's last few minutes at the pub. The secretary began crying as she disconnected Charlie's phone. Mr. Carter gave them both the remainder of the day off.

The rest of the staff had little energy and little enthusiasm for work. Charlie's colleagues felt apathy and indifference, as if they couldn't care what happened next. This happened to Judy Collins, as she describes in her book *The Seven T's: Finding Hope and Healing in the Wake of Tragedy*. She claims that after her son committed suicide, she found herself searching for ways of understanding what had happened in her life and how she was going to change her life.[4] Charlie's coworkers, who usually enjoyed high-energy levels in the office, now sat with blank faces trying to decide who was inheriting Charlie's responsibilities and work assignments. One employee had difficulty coping because on Charlie's folders he received as his share of office work he found penciled notes as well as doodles of smiling faces. He recognized Charlie's handwriting and it brought back memories. For the first two weeks after the funeral, the employee merely coasted. Frequently, they would gather in small groups around someone's desk to tell Charlie's stories. Little work was done.

A few days after the funeral, I had a chance to speak with four of these staff members. Two women shed tears with the mention of Charlie's name. The men I talked to wanted me to know what a sensitive and true friend he was to his colleagues.

Being Sensitive to Employee Needs

Usually, when a traumatic experience happens to an individual such as a death in the family, the workplace offers the person the opportunity to take bereavement leave and go to the EAP office to get one-on-one counseling. Some organizations even provide debriefing experts to talk with the individuals who have been affected by the trauma. We now understand that when they return to the workplace, managers and coworkers can support and promote the emotional recovery process.

The trauma of Charlie's death provided a similar, but quite different, situation. This was not a case of one survivor returning to the workplace after a trauma, but a close-knit team, including managers and coworkers, all of whom considered Charlie a close friend. Who would welcome *them* back to the office, prepare a welcome mat for them, and help them readjust?

Mr. Carter, the director, knew of my research, and called to talk about what had occurred in his office. The work he had done with his staff was effective and important, such as participating in the funeral, talking to his employees, being sensitive to their regular workloads and special assignments, and getting extensions on due dates from his own supervisor. He also sent a card signed by each of the office members to Charlie's family along with a book about loss and grief.

I pointed out that each person on his staff, including him, would be called a TLE employee. Together we reviewed the psychological stages of emotional recovery for people who have experienced a trauma and how he and the others there could help each other during their recovery by (1) putting out a welcome mat, (2) lending a listening ear to each other for retelling the trauma story, and (3) offering a helping hand to each other to help everyone get reconnected in their relationships at the workplace. Together, we discussed ways each of these stages could be of help to the staff—at least what he could do. This is what he did.

First, in putting out a welcome mat, he declared the office a safe haven for all his employees. He gave time off to those who needed it and did not force people to complete their work or meet deadlines. He realized this was not the time to be a taskmaster. He allowed them the freedom to choose to go for a walk or take frequent breaks from their normal activities. He met with each staff member to assure them their work assignment deadlines would be extended.

Second, Mr. Carter encouraged those employees who wanted to tell the trauma story to lend a listening ear to each other—or to him. Many of the employees took him up on his offer and stopped in to talk with him about Charlie. At the water cooler, colleagues reminisced and told stories about Charlie and said how much they missed him. Joanne, however, could not seem to talk about Charlie. Because she had witnessed the death of her dear friend and was still in shock, she was unable to share her feelings with her colleagues. One member of the budget team asked her to go for a walk. She purposely didn't ask Joanne about Charlie. Joanne found that to be helpful.

Mr. Carter felt that he could offer a helping hand in getting everyone reconnected, but it would take time. He delayed assignments and decided to honor Charlie's memory by dedicating the staff meeting room to him and naming it in his honor. He decided to have a special ceremony later in the year and invite Charlie's family to join his staff in honoring his memory. He let resuming normal workplace speed up to each staff person. "When you have the energy," was what he said to them. He knew that each person would react differently, and patience was needed to heal this wound. A major difficulty was passing out Charlie's assignments and clearing his office space.

Recommendation to Organizations

There are some important thoughts that should be conveyed to managers and organizations when reacting to the death of a coworker, especially when the entire staff is traumatized by the event.

First, it is *not* recommended to have a Dialogue Circle *after* the death of a coworker or manager, certainly not soon after. Charlie's case provided a clear example of this. The staff's grief was too tangibly present. Because of their state of shock, individuals would be unable to participate in and benefit from the group discussions. Returning TLE employees will most likely not yet have processed their grief feelings and will feel invaded if asked in a formal Dialogue Circle session to share any feelings about the loss of the coworker.

In some cases, a professional therapist or social worker may conduct a debriefing session with such a group of colleagues, but a debriefing session with its formal structure is different from a Dialogue Circle. Also, in observing the condition of traumatized coworkers, the manager may suggest one-on-one counseling, or a referral to the EAP of the organization, or to a member of the human resource staff.

Second, I suggest following Charlie's manager's example. He talked with all Charlie's coworkers individually. After a few months, workers may be ready to talk about Charlie's death in a Dialogue Circle setting. It is important to allow the office to reintegrate itself emotionally before assembling the staff in a structured educational setting to talk about the loss of their coworker.

Third, it is always a much better idea to prepare the staff before any crisis happens, while everything is calm and going smoothly. This is the time for an organization to take a proactive approach. Have a Dialogue Circle on this topic of healing from trauma *prior* to any traumatic events. In a less emotionally charged context, managers and coworkers can share past experiences and learn skills from each other on how to respond when a traumatized employee returns to the workplace. They would also be better prepared to cope and care for each other if a traumatic event happened to the whole group.

Notes

1. Jamie Marich, *Trauma Made Simple: Competencies in Assessment, Treatment and Working with Survivors* (Eau Claire, WI: PESI Publishing, 2014), 123.

2. Bessel van der Kolk, *The Body Keeps the Score: Brain, Mind, and Body in the Healing of Trauma* (New York: Viking Press, 2014), 204.

3. George A. Bonanno, *The Other Side of Sadness: What the New Science of Bereavement Tells Us about Life after Loss* (New York: Basic Books, 2009), 109.

4. Judy Collins, *The Seven T's: Finding Hope and Healing in the Wake of Tragedy* (New York: Penguin, 2007), 103.

~

CHAPTER FOURTEEN

What Challenges Does a Facilitator Face?

Questions and Sensitive Topics

It's important to note that even before the first Dialogue Circle session you, as the facilitator, may be challenged by questions from participants as to the importance of the topic and the need to engage in a dialogue about a sensitive topic such as trauma. Here are a few common questions and challenges that you may hear from participants of your Dialogue Circle—and the ways I might respond to them.

Why do I need to be here?
It's important to point out to the participants that the subject of an employee returning to the workplace after a traumatic experience involves all sectors of the organization—both employee and managerial personnel. *This must be stressed.* Everyone in the workplace either has had a TLE, or is close to someone who has been through a transition that involved a trauma. This Dialogue Circle will help participants become more sensitive to the needs of a TLE employee returning to the workplace.

How will I learn?
In a Dialogue Circle, participants all learn from each other. The active exchange of ideas and the experiences that are shared during each session create an environment of curiosity, mutual enrichment, and learning. What really needs to be learned in the Dialogue Circle on TLEs will be learned through the sharing of experiences.

How will this Dialogue Circle help me do my job better?
This Dialogue Circle will make you more aware of employees when they return to the workplace after having experienced a trauma in their life. During the sessions, you will hear comments from both managers and employees. This shared experience with others and your own personal experience will enable you to understand and respond to the TLE employee better.

As a manager, how will this Dialogue Circle make me more effective?
Hopefully, you will become more aware of your important role in dealing with returning TLE employees. What others expect of you will be reflected through the words of the employees who will give feedback on the trauma issues that emerge. Because of their insights, you will communicate better with a returning TLE employee, and you will be able to identify the stages of trauma recovery as they unfold in such people.

As an employee, what information will I take back to the office that will make my relationships with my colleagues better?
You will gain helpful information about relating to an individual who has just returned to the workplace after having experienced a trauma: how to approach that person and what to say to welcome the employee back to work appropriately.

How will the organization benefit from people participating in this Dialogue Circle?
A change in attitude and behavior toward the returning TLE employee will begin happening throughout your organization. It will have a positive effect on employee cooperation and productivity.

Challenges

Most Dialogue Circles run smoothly because participants who volunteer want to learn more about this topic. However, from time to time an individual's behavior or verbal comments may cause some slight disruptions during a session. Some of these behaviors can be expected around sensitive topics, as group exchanges become intense with different personalities interacting and diverse opinions surfacing. Any of the following situations may occur during Dialogue Circle sessions and may need to be addressed by the facilitator.

> *Situation:* An employee in the Dialogue Circle does not want to talk or share personal experiences.

Response: Don't make participants feel uncomfortable by insisting that they share their personal experience. If a participant does not want to share, the facilitator simply moves on with the discussion or asks another participant to talk about his or her experience. A nonjudgmental approach is best in this situation, since the resistant participant may have good reasons for not discussing certain personal points.

Situation: A participant consistently dominates, interrupts, or monopolizes the session with personal experiences and stories.

Response: Sometimes in groups we encounter individuals who have a great need to talk, thus preventing other people from getting their share of group time. As a session progresses, the group will usually become less tolerant of such an individual who always wants to talk or interrupts others. A person who exhibits this type of behavior needs to be gently challenged to look at the effects of their behavior. You, as the facilitator, can gently confront the person and say, "Let's focus on another person's experience for a while." Or, you may confront the participant by saying something like: "Sally, you appear to share easily. I notice you typically identify with most of the problems that have been raised in the group. Is there anything special that you want us to know about you? Otherwise, there are others who would like to speak." This intervention will give Sally an opportunity to gracefully stop. If she continues to monopolize the session, the facilitator can talk with her privately during a break.

Situation: Suppose a participant begins to cry during a session, as can be expected in the second session when persons relate their trauma stories.

Response: Allow the participant to cry. Comfort the participant yourself, either verbally or by a gentle touch, if someone else in the group has not already done so. Assure him or her that it is okay to cry. Continue on with the Dialogue Circle.

Situation: Suppose a participant in the Dialogue Circle starts criticizing or blaming other participants as they tell their story, thereby creating a disruption in the group.

Response: Participants should be advised at the beginning of the Dialogue that this is a learning experience for everyone and it's important to maintain a learning environment. If the critical person does not heed this advice, the facilitator might want to have a private conversation with the participant after the session.

Difficult Questions

If the participant asks the facilitator a question to which the facilitator does not know the answer, the facilitator should acknowledge the question and promise to find the answer and get back to them at a specific time, for example, in an hour or at the next session.

I recall once that a participant asked me about some form of therapy for traumatized people he had heard was being used on an employee. I had never heard of this therapeutic intervention, told him so, and promised to find out about it and report back to the group. I did so, and in my research found many new approaches that psychologists and psychiatrists were using to foster recovery in traumatized patients. I found my research so interesting that I thought readers of this book might like to know about them too. I reported on some of these in chapter 6, "What Does Psychology Tell Us about Trauma?"

Also, many times in a well-planned session something may go wrong and there may be some time constraints that may keep the discussion from moving forward. The session may have been late getting started, the discussion may get sidetracked from the topic for a time, someone in the group may get emotionally upset recalling a traumatic experience and need to be cared for, or you may have a group where everyone wants to tell their story and each one's story is quite long and involved.

The facilitator may bring the issue of a lack of time to the group's attention and the content they need to cover. Then, the facilitator adjusts by moving quickly through certain portions of the discussion, watching the clock to ensure having an appropriate amount of time for processing the session.

Resistant Participants

If an organization makes the Dialogue Circle a requirement for managers and employees, some employees may not want to participate because they may think it is an inconvenience, imposition, invasion of their privacy, or robs them of their work or lunch time. If this happens, there may be some questions about resistance to participating. Here are some common forms of resistance:

- *I really don't want to be here. I feel this is just a waste of my time.*
- *We have been okay dealing with this problem before in our office.*
- *How are you going to make things easier for me by requiring me to attend a Dialogue Circle?*
- *Do I have to change my whole personality to take care of this returning TLE employee?*
- *I'd rather not deal with him.*
- *Does this mean that I won't have to go to the EAP when I have a problem?*

Here are some suggested ways to respond:

- If the participant is adamant about not wanting to attend, perhaps you can speak to his supervisor and have him excused. The best participants are those who attend willingly. A few angry and resentful participants can ruin a Dialogue Circle.
- If the participant is merely hedging about attending the sessions, he or she may simply need some encouragement such as, "Every participant has said how helpful and useful the sessions were. You'd probably enjoy being part of the group."
- Suggest to the participant to talk to a colleague who has participated in a Dialogue Circle to get some feedback as to the nature of the dialogue and interaction.

Facilitator Expectations

Most of my Dialogue Circle groups consist of managers and employees with no specific interpersonal skill base. They attend the sessions primarily because of availability and referral. Invariably, the group "chemistry" turns out to be excellent. Participants get along exceptionally well and freely share their experiences with each other. These groups seem also to enjoy light humor and no one seems to upstage another participant.

After facilitating a number of these Dialogue Circles on managing workplace trauma, I began to have certain expectations of the Dialogue Circle process. For example, I expected the group to develop a trusting cohesion, if not during the first session, certainly by the second. Sometimes, my expectations were not fulfilled.

I once had a group of participants most of whom happened to be experts in their fields: one was an alternative dispute resolution expert, two were lawyers, two were labor relations executives, two were workshop leaders and trainers, and two were human resources managers. During Pre–Dialogue Circle interviews, each of these participants shared not only their trauma stories, but also information about their careers and life experiences. But during the Dialogue Circle itself they remained silent about their personal traumas.

When the actual sessions began, I fully expected that because these individuals were seasoned managers—even though some knew each other, and some did not—they would come together as a group with excellent group dynamics. This did not happen.

Instead, no "chemistry" seemed to develop in the group. Except for a few—and hesitantly—they did not share their trauma experiences publicly in the group, even though privately they had told me about them in detail. I found this a puzzling situation. What I soon realized was that this group of experts were used to being presenters and team leaders, not participants. They were used to being up front, on stage. They saw themselves as the ones expected to have the answers, to give advice and direction to others. They were not used to revealing themselves as vulnerable, especially in front of each other. And they seemed unwilling to change their public image.

The more ordinary employees in the group were swayed and perhaps awed by these experts, and so hesitated to offer opinions or disagree. Because the experts were all seen as having "power" in their "career roles," they influenced the others to agree on what managerial skills were needed in dealing with a returning TLE employee.

These experts seemed most concerned with teaching the other participants and promoting the value of listening skills. Over and over, they pointed out how managers needed to be trained and skilled in good communication and active listening skills, but ironically, as representative of these skills, they did not "walk their talk."

Although they were all certified as experts in group process, their technical skills did not appear to help them in the Dialogue Circle sessions. Their skills seemed to inhibit them from "opening up" and "sharing" their own life and trauma experiences. It looked like these same people were "posturing and pontificating" during the sessions, as one employee pointed out. Their advice in the group was directed outward and not inward toward themselves.

I wondered whether these experts would create a "welcome environment" for a returning TLE employee, since they were unable to do it among the group in the Dialogue Circle sessions.

In cases like these, as a facilitator, keep in mind important elements for facilitating, according to Roger M. Schwarz in his new edition of his book *The Skilled Facilitator*.

They are as follows:

- The whole group is the facilitator's client. The facilitator is not a group member and cannot focus all the group's attention on certain members at the expense of others.
- The main tasks of the facilitator are to increase group effectiveness. Here, staying focused on content and process is important to help the group become more successful.

- Facilitators must remain neutral and allow the group to solve their problems.
- Facilitators need to promote an atmosphere of mutual learning, allowing the group to create a productive mindset for interaction and greater individual well-being.[1]

Realizing that cohesion was not happening after the first session with this highly sophisticated group, I was not sure what to do. So, I continued following the Dialogue Circle process and, even though the group never did develop a strong cohesion, everyone managed to profit much from the sessions. Evaluations assured me that the Dialogue Circle had been useful and practical for just about everyone. But because these managers refused to share their stories and life experiences during the second and last sessions, I felt this Dialogue Circle provided a poorer learning experience for that group, especially since I knew the richness of all their stories from the Pre–Dialogue Circle interviews.

I also realized it is important for the facilitator to be aware that the kinds of individuals recruited for the sessions will make a difference in the quality and tone of the Dialogue Circle. For example, if you recruit a group of engineers, their technical expertise may bias views on how to approach a returning TLE employee. A similar biased result may occur if you find yourself facilitating a group entirely of counselors or group process–oriented people.

Another important observation concerns self-disclosure. The closest and most meaningful relationships that humans enjoy involve self-disclosure. Self-disclosure is not meant to make people feel more separate or alone, it is meant to do the opposite. It frequently brings coworkers and friends closer. During the second session in the group with all the "experts" I asked an employee in the group to tell her trauma story. This was a conscious decision on my part to try to create more "sharing." To prime the pump, as it were. It worked, but only to get the other employees in the group to tell their stories; the experts did not follow suit.

Note

1. Roger M. Schwarz, *The Skilled Facilitator: A Comprehensive Resource for Consultants, Facilitators, Managers, Trainers and Coaches* (Hoboken, NJ: Wiley, 2017), 28.

CHAPTER FIFTEEN

~

Helping Yourself after a Traumatic Life Experience

Self-Help as an Intervention

Any TLE employee can easily find an abundance of books, magazines, and other publications written to provide guidance and support to individuals who have experienced a range of traumas. All bookstores now have a "self-help" section where you can select from a menu of general and specific publications. Many of these books provide insights applicable to TLEs.

One self-help publication which has applicability to a broad range of symptoms exhibited by trauma victims is *Minding the Body, Mending the Mind* by Joan Borysenko, PhD. She challenges us to "wholeness" and "healing." She explains,

> To be whole means to be a flexible adventurer, ready to meet life's challenges with engagement and curiosity. It means feeling a sense of connection to the whole of life—to other people, to new ideas, to the world around us. It means thinking less about "I, me, and mine" and more about how we are all interconnected in a great web of life. It means caring for others and doing what we can to make the world a better place. It means recognizing that happiness arises within us *independent* of any external cause and removing the obstructions to that inner peace and happiness that are our birthright as human beings.
>
> Whether you are healthy or sick, young or old, rich or poor, you can still be happy and optimize your physical function. That's what minding the body and mending the mind are all about.[1]

Carol S. Dweck, PhD, is the author of the successful book *Mindset: The New Psychology of Success: How We Can Learn to Fulfill Our Potential.* Building on over twenty years research, she has shown that

> *the view you adopt for yourself* profoundly affects the way you lead your life. It can determine whether you become the person you want to be and whether you accomplish the things you value. How does this happen? How can a simple belief have the power to transform your psychology and, as a result, your life?
>
> Believing that your qualities are carved in stone—the *fixed mindset*—creates an urgency to prove yourself over and over. If you have only a certain amount of intelligence, a certain personality, and a certain moral character—well, then you'd better prove that you have a healthy dose of them. It simply wouldn't do to look or feel deficient in these most basic characteristics.[2]

A "fixed mindset" person believes that their talents are fixed and can't be changed or improved. You are who you are—your abilities are fixed, so you should not seek challenges.

However, the opposite of the "fixed mindset" is the "growth mindset" where your abilities can flourish and be developed. This mindset is ongoing. One can have a lifelong passion for learning and for personal improvement. A growth mindset will continually stretch you. Dr. Dweck has applied her research to organizations, relationships, and athletes where she feels that abilities can be developed.

Kristin Neff, PhD and author of *Self-Compassion: The Proven Power of Being Kind to Yourself*, states that we are living in a highly competitive society and it is hard to feel good about ourselves. We tend to judge ourselves harshly and at times our self-talk produces negative effects in ourselves. She proposes developing *self-compassion*, which entails three core components. The first is,

> *self-kindness*—that we be gentle and understanding with ourselves rather than harshly critical and judgmental. Second, it requires recognition of our *common humanity*, feeling connected with others in the experience of life rather than feeling isolated and alienated by our suffering. Third, it requires *mindfulness*— that we hold our experience in balanced awareness, rather than ignoring our pain nor exaggerating it. We must achieve and combine these three essential elements in order to be truly self-compassionate.[3]

In addition to striving to be more compassionate with ourselves and with each other, there are other behaviors we need to integrate and cultivate if we wish to live a wholesome life.

Brené Brown, PhD, in her book *The Gifts of Imperfection: Let Go of Who You Think You're Supposed to Be and Embrace Who You Are*, quotes ee cummings on authenticity: "To be nobody-but-yourself in a world which is doing its best, night and day, to make you everybody but yourself—means to fight the hardest battle which any human being can fight—and never stop fighting." "Staying real" is one of the most courageous battles that we'll ever fight.[4]

It is a daily struggle to be ourselves when we are up against individuals who challenge us and our values and question us when they see us changing. We have to learn to stick to our values and know how to set boundaries, since they will always be challenged. Brown says,

> Sacrificing who we are for the sake of what other people think just isn't worth it. Yes, there can be authenticity growing pains for the people around us, but in the end, being true to ourselves is the best gift we can give the people we love.[5]

Feeling Good: The New Mood Therapy by David Burns, MD, is another wonderful reference book that has wide application in fostering recovery from trauma. He suggests a multitude of resources on topics related to growth and change. Burns proposed cognitive therapy as a self-help tool to help change your mood. By "cognitive" he means how you are thinking and feeling about things at a particular moment. His approach is quite simple.

If you are in a depressed and anxious mood, you are most likely thinking in an illogical, negative manner and you will consequently tend to make unhelpful decisions and behave in a self-defeating manner. With some effort and practice you can train yourself to straighten your thinking patterns. Then, as the negative thinking is eliminated, your mood will lift, you will become more productive and happy again, and you will respect yourself. This transformation can be accomplished in a relatively short period of time.

According to Burns, your moods are created by your own cognition or thoughts—the way you look at things and the way you interpret things. He calls this approach "fast acting." Once you eliminate the negative thinking, he says you can alter any mood.[6]

This process does not, of course, eliminate the effects of the traumatic experience. It is not designed to heal the body or the short-circuited memories caused by the trauma, but it can help you shift your mood, if you have the patience and discipline to follow Burns's instructions.

Another important point to be made about self-help books is self-esteem. Countless books have been written about this subject. Our thought process controls the way we function. What we feed into our brain and our memory determines how we act and behave toward our community, toward our peers, and in our relationships. For example, I recall when I was trying to figure out what college I wanted to attend. I was confused. Around that time, I went to the library and came across a book by Claude Bristol titled *The Magic of Believing: The Science of Setting Your Goal and Then Reaching It*. This is an old book but people still refer to it and it still sits on bookstore shelves. I keep this book in my personal library. It emphasizes goal-setting. It helped me focus and clarify what I wanted to do with my life and where I wanted to go to college. I still practice what I learned from it.

I encourage individuals to read self-help books. They can assist you in defining a personal goal and help you carve out a new road ahead for yourself.

Dr. Louis Savary and Dr. Patricia Berne, in their book *You Are God's Gift to the World: The Purpose of Your Life on Earth*, takes a more spiritual look at self-help. They cite Dr. Mehmet Oz, the famous physician and television personality. He says,

> Finding and having a purpose in life that is of service to others is one big secret to enjoying good health. I've performed open-heart surgeries for 17 years and I repeatedly hear the same post-op request from a patient's worried spouse, "Please tell my hard-charging significant other to retire." And not once have I done it, no matter how reasonable the request. That's because I believe, deeply that having a purpose in your life is the key to good health.[7]

Savary and Berne comment,

> Having a purpose doesn't stop with retirement. As long as you are still breathing, you have a purpose. Having a purpose for living is good not only for your personal physical and mental health but also for the health of our planet and for the success of God's work in the world.
>
> Notice that, though for some people their job or occupation may be part of their purpose or destiny, your life purpose is always much larger and broader than any job. Dr. Oz's recommendation was not that heart attack survivors should keep working for the same company till the day they die, but that no matter where people were in life they need to find a purpose, someplace where their contribution can make a positive difference.[8]

I have dedicated this book to my parents. My father had a purpose in his life. He was both the tax collector in our community and he umpired baseball. He died of lung cancer at the age of eighty-nine. However, he umpired baseball until he barely could stand behind home plate, and he collected taxes in our community for forty-two years. He served his community well and was a wonderful role model for my brother and me. He never thought of retiring. That word was not in his vocabulary. He was full of life and always eager to see what the next day would bring. His purpose in life was to live his life to the fullest—and he did.

In the last half century self-help books have grown to a cultural growth in our nation. These books have witnessed an expansion of topics, resources, and people. But they are not your only available resource.

Specialized Support Groups

You can also join a self-help group specific to your type of traumatic experience, whether you are coping with a certain developmental disability, chronic emotional problem, an addiction, terminal illness, or a specific traumatic life event such as a divorce or death of a family member. There is probably a self-help group in your area that would welcome you.

Participants in these groups are usually individuals who share a common troubling situation and who willingly serve as helpers to assist other people, perhaps by providing information about the issue or by engaging in constructive actions with them.

Self-help groups do not provide therapy, but focus on peer support and education in their area of concern. There you will meet people like yourself who have had traumatic experiences like yourself. These groups are usually available at low or no cost. Counselors and therapists often suggest that their clients participate in a self-help group to cope more effectively with their specific problems.

Self-help books can be purchased both offline and online. Between 1972 and 2000, the numbers of self-help books increased from 1.1 percent to 2.4 percent of the total number of books in print. These books focus on popular psychology topics such as romantic relationships, or aspects of the mind and human behavior. Self-help books typically advertise themselves as being able to increase self-awareness and performance, including satisfaction with one's life.

Notes

1. Joan Borysenko, *Minding the Body, Mending the Mind* (Cambridge, MA: Perseus Group, 2008), 33–34.

2. Carol S. Dweck, *Mindset: The New Psychology of Success: How We Can Learn to Fulfill Our Potential* (New York: Ballantine Books, 2008), 6.

3. Kristin Neff, *Self-Compassion: The Proven Power of Being Kind to Yourself* (New York: William Morrow, 2011), 41.

4. Brené Brown, *The Gifts of Imperfection: Let Go of Who You Think You're Supposed to Be and Embrace Who You Are* (Center City, MN: Hazelden, 2010), 51.

5. Brown, *The Gifts of Imperfection*, 53.

6. David Burns, *Feeling Good: The New Mood Therapy* (New York: HarperCollins, 1999), 12.

7. Louis M. Savary and Patricia H. Berne, *You Are God's Gift to the World: The Purpose of Your Life on Earth* (Bloomington, IN: Balboa Press, 2013), ix.

8. Savary and Berne, *You Are God's Gift to the World*.

CHAPTER SIXTEEN

Children of Traumatized Employees

We usually hear of a TLE happening directly to an individual, but its powerful effects may radiate to others. These others may be colleagues or coworkers as when someone is attacked in the office building where they work, or someone is unexpectedly dismissed from a job. More often, however, a personal trauma, whether it happens at work or elsewhere, is likely to have a strong effect in the home, touching all members of a family, especially the younger children. Psychologists are discovering that children are easily upset emotionally by a traumatic event experienced by a parent or sibling, yet may not show it directly or overtly. This chapter offers some perspectives on this issue.

Although what happens to children after a parent is traumatized is not explicitly the responsibility of people in the workplace, it may be helpful for managers and other employees to know the kinds of things that may be going on in the children of TLEs employee returning to work. Because a TLE puts unusual stress on the survivor's entire family, the information in these few pages is important. The knowledge may be helpful in giving support, in knowing what to expect or watch for in a child's thoughts and behavior, and in knowing what to say and what not to say to the parent.

It's also important since returning TLE employees may need extra time off and support in helping their children process the traumatic events and deal with their own feelings or reactions. For example, the parent may need to personally take the child to school for a time and pick the child up after school.

Psychologists tell us that when a child's parent or sibling dies, either naturally or accidentally, a number of thoughts are likely to occupy the child's mind.

First, *the child may somehow feel responsible for the death of the family member.* This may seem strange to most adults, but psychologists remind us that the child's mind is not logical. Some children believe that wishing for something makes that thing happen. So, children may think that the death (or serious illness, a divorce, or some other unwelcome event) happened because they had angry feelings toward the person who died, or that the death was punishment for certain bad behaviors they did, or that there was something they could have done to prevent the death, especially if the death was accidental.

Freddie's mother was killed in an auto accident driving him to school. So, not only was eight-year-old Freddie a witness to her death, he also blamed himself for her death because he was late getting dressed that morning and his mother had to hurry to get him to school. If he had been on time, he told himself over and over, his mother would still be alive, and therefore her death is his fault and he is to blame. Children like Freddie need to be reassured that they were not responsible for the trauma and, in his case, that he was not driving the car or in charge of how his mother drove. He needs to hear that her death was not his fault.

Jennifer's grandfather lived with her family and was dying of cancer. Frequently, she would get angry at him because he complained a lot and snored loudly at night keeping her awake. He died during a night when, earlier that evening, ten-year-old Jennifer had angry and hateful feelings toward him, wishing he were no longer in their house. She felt sure her anger was really a wish for his death, and she concluded that somehow she had caused his death and was responsible for it. Jennifer needs to know that her feelings and wishes did not cause her grandfather's death, that nothing she did or didn't do could have made things come out differently.

When children have guilty thoughts like these after a TLE has happened to someone close to them, children need to be reminded, perhaps again and again that:

- They were not at fault.
- There was nothing they could have done to make it come out differently.
- They were not responsible for the situation, nor were they in charge of it.

And, if the family is religious, they can assure the child that the person who died is being taken care of by God and is happy.

A Sense of Security

When something dire happens—death of a parent, divorce, burglary—children feel very insecure. Someone who has been their protector is either gone or appears inadequate to the task of keeping them safe.

Grief is the normal response to sorrow and confusion that comes from losing someone or something important to you. It is a typical reaction to death, divorce, job loss, a move to another town, or a loss of health. There is also an important normal emotional response in children when that loss triggers fear for their safety, security, and protection. Children, for all their bravado, are fragile beings who need to be cared for and protected. They cannot really take care of themselves and they cannot survive on their own, and they know it at a gut level.

David's father, an executive with a large manufacturing firm, had a sudden heart attack and died almost immediately. Afterward, he heard his mother in her room sobbing and crying aloud, "Who will take care of us now?" Five-year-old David began to grow anxious that he and his mother would be thrown out of their house and have to live homeless and hungry from now on. Anxiety and depression are contagious emotions, especially for children.

When Geraldine's father divorced her mother, he was very angry and she overheard him tell her mother that he no longer loved her. Geraldine, who was only four, interpreted this to mean that her father also no longer loved her either. Children of divorce, like Geraldine, need to be reassured that they are not at fault, that they did nothing to cause the divorce, and that both parents love them as much as ever.

Raoul's home was broken into one afternoon while he was in school and both his parents were at work. Raoul, a fourth grader, was upset seeing his home ransacked, and for the next few nights had nightmares about his house being attacked with him inside. The one place he had counted on for feeling safe, his home, was no longer safe. Raoul needs to be reassured that everything is being done to ensure the future safety of the family home.

At times like these, children need to be reassured that, despite the TLE that happened,

- They are loved.
- They are safe and will be protected.
- They will be cared for.

In such cases, children like Geraldine and David, in the wake of the traumatic experience, often fear that more separation and abandonment will happen to them. Filled with "separation anxiety" they may not want to leave the house and may not want the remaining parent to leave either. A loving adult may have to take time off work to be close to anxious children for a certain period. For example, the adult may have to spend much more quality time with such children.

Some children affected by a trauma that happened to a parent may develop anxiety strong enough to require professional help from a counselor or therapist. Children quickly pick up on parental feelings. (Any parent can tell you that when he or she is having a bad day, that is when children will begin acting out, possibly acting out the feelings of the parent.)

After being affected by a trauma, you may notice that the child consciously avoids any activities or symbols that remind them of the original trauma or the person traumatized. The child may hide or even break a photo of the divorcing parent or of a family member who died. Or the opposite may happen. The child may become preoccupied with symbols of the person traumatized and begin kissing the photo or putting it in a prominent place in his or her room.

Typical Signs in Children Affected by a Traumatic Event

When a traumatic event occurs in a family, psychologists tell us that they look for some of the following typical signs that children have been strongly affected by the trauma. The child may:

- become quiet and withdrawn
- show a change in appetite
- feel and act depressed
- become jumpy and irritable
- report unexplained illnesses
- have unprovoked outbursts of anger
- become anxious or fearful
- no longer show interest in things that he or she used to find interesting
- have difficulty concentrating or completing tasks
- have trouble going to sleep or have nightmares[1]

Psychologists tell us that most of these symptoms displayed by children are normal and will usually dissipate after a time, when children are reassured that they were not responsible for the traumatic event and they are loved, safe, and well cared for.

The Need for Professional Counseling

If some of these symptoms persist or have excessive manifestation, professional counseling is recommended. For example, after being affected by a traumatic event, it is normal for a child to become quiet and withdrawn, but if the child seems to remain estranged and totally detached from all other people, the child may need professional help.

It is also normal for a child touched by trauma to feel depressed for a time, but if the child manifests a "numbness of feelings," where there is little or no affect and no sign of a lifting mood, the child may be suffering what professional call "emotional anesthesia" and need help to overcome it.

While it is normal for a child affected by a traumatic loss to be anxious and fearful for a time, it is not normal for the child to continue for weeks and months being hyper-vigilant and giving exaggerated startle responses.

While it is typical for a child, after a trauma happens in a family, to report unexplained illnesses like stomachaches, it is not typical for such a child to begin making suicidal statements. Moreover, if the recurring aches and pains do not respond to household treatment and some tender loving care, seek help from a doctor.

While a child, recovering from a traumatic happening to a parent or sibling, may have difficulty concentrating on homework or completing household chores for a time, it is unusual for such a child, when asked what he wants to be when he grows up, not to see himself as ever having a future.

How Does Grief Differ from Depression?

Grief is a normal experience. Shortly after a death or a loss, people—adults and children—may feel empty or numb, as if in shock. They may notice physical changes such as trembling, nausea, muscle weakness, dry mouth, shortness of breath, or trouble sleeping and eating. Emotionally, they may feel an unexplainable anger welling up at a particular person, at a certain situation, or at nothing they can identify. They may feel guilty, saying things to themselves like, "I could have said . . ." or "I should have done . . . " or "I wish I had tried to . . . " People in grief may have strange dreams or nightmares. Socially they may become absent-minded, avoid friends, not want to return to work. These are the typical physical, social, and emotional responses to grief. Because they are normal to the grieving period, they will pass as the grief does.

Depression is something more than the feeling of grief after losing someone or something you cherish. Clinical depression is a disorder of the entire person. Though depression may begin with grief, the symptoms of depression don't stop or lessen. They get worse and become an illness that can take over the way a person thinks and feels. When a child is truly depressed, the child becomes, almost, another person.

When the child's symptoms of grief don't subside, but grow in intensity, it is time to seek professional help. If you observe the signs of depression in an adult or child, recommend that they see a doctor or a therapist.

Summary

When children experience a crisis situation, are impacted by a traumatic event, or suffer a personal loss through death of a loved one, they begin to learn that the world they live in is not always reliable. But they also learn that, when traumatic things happen, people come together to console and help each other. Adult human beings can demonstrate to children the power of the human spirit to live through and even transcend tragedy. Children who have healthy models can learn to cope effectively and are more likely to build a strong sense of self-esteem. So when life deals them crushing blows, they can say to themselves, "I can get over it." And they do.

However, there are some instances when tragedy strikes and a different type of story evolves. An unusual story is told by author Sue Klebold in her book *A Mother's Reckoning: Living in the Aftermath of Tragedy*. Ms. Klebold illuminates the trauma of her son Dylan Klebold and Eric Harris. These two young men killed twelve students and a teacher, and wounded twenty-four others, before taking their own lives. This tragedy happened in Columbine High School in Littleton, Colorado, on April 20, 1999. This mother details how she coped with this family trauma and how she struggled as a TLE going back to work in a state of sheer panic, having another son at home (Byron) whom she feared would take his own life.[2]

She wrote about how she worried he'd harm himself. It was a terribly unfair position to put him in. "I was asking him to reassure me he was okay—really, I was asking him to *be* okay—when of course he was not. It would take a long time for us to talk about our devastation while assuring one another we were still committed to life."[3]

Accumulated leave at the local community college gave Ms. Klebold an opportunity to use this time to deal with the family trauma. When it came time for her to return to work and negotiate her workplace reentry, her supervisor was supportive. They agreed on a project where she could work part time at home and part time at work. A memo was sent to the staff upon her return.

However, when she returned she described feeling fragile and scared because of the media coverage. But she was warmly greeted by staff people. She said, "Although I did not realize it at the time, returning to work provided an essential framework for my recovery on many levels . . . it allowed me to experience directly the compassion and sympathy other people were capable of."[4]

As a returning TLE, Sue Klebold allowed herself to experience warmth from her fellow employees. Her coworkers hugged her and she welcomed their embrace. They walked a fine line showing sensitivity to her situation while putting out a welcoming mat for her.

Notes

1. These same symptoms are also characteristically found in adults affected by the trauma.

2. Sue Klebold, *A Mother's Reckoning: Living in the Aftermath of Tragedy* (New York: Broadway Books, 2017).

3. Klebold, *A Mother's Reckoning*, 94.

4. Klebold, *A Mother's Reckoning*, 115.

~

Appendix

The Role of the Participant

Participants in a Dialogue Circle are its most important elements. Their commitment, eagerness, and interest are essential in making the Dialogue Circle a success.

It is important for Dialogue Circle facilitators to point out to participants that handout material does not have to be memorized, there are no difficult concepts to comprehend, and there will be no test afterward. Rather, encourage participants to focus on their interactions with each other. Listening to each other's experience is the way they will gain a deep understanding of the topic. The process—an open democratic dialogue with colleagues—is an important part of the Dialogue Circle experience.

The following points adapted from *The Study Circle Handbook: A Manual for Study Circle, Discussion Leaders, Organizers and Participants* (Study Circles Resource Center 1993) will assist those participating in a Study Circle:

1. *Make a commitment to attend all Dialogue Circle sessions.* Each Dialogue Circle creates its own culture and getting to know the people with whom you will spend this time is part of the ongoing learning experience of a Dialogue Circle.
2. *Be willing to share your thoughts and feelings with others.* Share your perceptions and suggestions with the group and ask for clarification of others' experiences when issues are not clear. Even though you may feel alone in your experience, you may be helping the group by sharing it.

3. *Keep the discussions focused.* Try not to bring in other ideas or topics that have no relevance to what is being discussed in your Dialogue Circle. But don't hesitate to bring in relevant points for discussion.

4. *Speak to the group.* When making your remarks, address the entire group, not just the leader/facilitator. Feel free to engage directly in dialogue with other participants. Everyone learns from interactions among the group members.

5. *Listen to others.* Give everyone a chance to speak and be heard. If you have a question for a group member, don't hesitate to ask the person to elaborate on a specific point. Also, be aware that some people may not be as assertive as others and may need time to come forward with their thoughts.

6. *Speak up.* Don't hesitate to engage in the Dialogue Circle discussion; however, be sensitive not to monopolize the discussion. Encourage others to participate and express their points of view.

7. *Don't withdraw from the group.* Each person in the Dialogue Circle brings unique skills and experiences to the topic. It's important to draw on these experiences during the Dialogue Circle sessions. Not participating keeps the whole group from learning what you know.

8. *Welcome friendly disagreement.* Conflict among participants is not discouraged. We all learn when people disagree and share their opinions with the group. Ideas can be challenged and individuals can be the catalyst in the group for bringing up new ideas. However, it is important that group emotions not get out of hand.

9. *Use humor.* Your personality is key in the group participation. If humor can be used to lighten up a session, it is encouraged. Be aware of your body language and the body language of others.

10. *Keep an open mind.* Your participation is appreciated when you come to each Dialogue Circle with an open mind to learning and engaging others. Don't hesitate to engage others in a dialogue about points that may need clarification or an idea that you may want to discuss.

11. *Use your critical faculties.* Think about what is being said in the sessions. It's important for you to keep a critical eye on statements made by authors of readings, the leader/facilitator, or other participants. Don't allow yourself to be intimidated by false assertions.

12. *Be open to other points of view.* It's important to understand another person's point of view, before outwardly criticizing that individual. They usually have a very good reason why they do not see a situation the same way you do. If you show empathy and understanding, many times your point of view will be heard with a different ear.

Select Bibliography

Bonanno, George A. *The Other Side of Sadness: What the New Science of Bereavement Tells Us about Life after Loss.* New York: Basic Books, 2009.

Borysenko, Joan. *It's Not the End of the World: Developing Resilience in Times of Change.* New York: Hay House, 2009.

———. *Minding the Body, Mending the Mind.* Cambridge, MA: Da Capo Press, 2007.

Boss, Pauline. *Loss, Trauma, and Resilience: Therapeutic Work with Ambiguous Loss.* New York: W. W. Norton, 2006.

Brown, Brené. *The Gifts of Imperfection: Let Go of Who You Think You're Supposed to Be and Embrace Who You Are.* Center City, MN: Hazelden, 2010.

———. *Rising Strong: The Reckoning, The Rumble, The Revolution.* New York: Spiegel & Grau, 2015.

Burns, David. *Feeling Good: The New Mood Therapy.* New York: HarperCollins, 1999.

Collins, Judy. *The Seven T's: Finding Hope and Healing in the Wake of Tragedy.* New York: Penguin, 2007.

Doverspike, William F. "Grief: The Journey from Suffering to Resilience." *Georgia Psychological Association* (2014): 1.

Dweck, Carol S. *Mindset: The New Psychology of Success, How We Can Learn to Fulfill Our Potential.* New York: Ballantine Books, 2008.

Fredrickson, Barbara L. *Positivity: Top-Notch Research Reveals the 3-to-1 Ratio That Will Change Your Life.* New York: Three Rivers Press, 2009.

Frost, Peter J. *Toxic Emotion at Work: How Compassionate Managers Handle Pain and Conflict.* Boston, MA: Harvard Business School Press, 2003.

Fryer, Bronwyn. "Compassion Management." *Harvard Business Review* (2013): 1–2.

Goleman, Daniel. *Social Intelligence: The Revolutionary New Science of Human Relationships.* New York: Bantam Books, 2006.

Haneberg, Lisa. *Focus Like a Laser Beam—10 Ways to Do What Matters Most.* San Francisco, Jossey-Bass, 2006.

Heller, Laurence, and Aline LaPierre. *Dealing with Developmental Trauma: How Early Trauma Affects Self-Regulation, Self-Image, and the Capacity for Relationship.* Berkeley, CA: North Atlantic Books, 2012.

Ingram, David. "Effective Group Communication." Retrieved from smallbusiness. chron.com/effective-group-communication-processes-3187.html.

Jeffreys, J. Shep. *Healing Grieving People When Tears Are Not Enough: A Handbook for Care Providers.* New York: Brunner-Routledge, 2005.

Klebold, Sue. *A Mother's Reckoning: Living in the Aftermath of Tragedy.* New York: Broadway Books, 2017.

Kosminsky, Phyllis. *Getting Back to Life When Grief Won't Heal.* New York: McGraw-Hill, 2007.

Levine, Peter A. *In an Unspoken Voice: How the Body Releases Trauma and Restores Goodness.* Berkeley, CA: North Atlantic Books, 2010.

Lubit, Roy. H. *Coping with Toxic Managers, Subordinates and Other Difficult People.* New York: Prentice Hall, 2004.

Lyubomirsky, Sonja. *The How of Happiness: A New Approach to Getting the Life You Want.* New York: Penguin, 2007.

Marich, Jamie. *Trauma Made Simple: Competencies in Assessment, Treatment and Working with Survivors.* Eau Claire, WI: PESI Publishing, 2014.

McLaren, Karla. *The Art of Empathy: A Complete Guide to Life's Most Essential Skill.* Boulder, CO: Sounds True, 2013.

Neff, Kristin, *Self-Compassion: The Proven Power of Being Kind to Yourself.* New York: William Morrow, 2011.

Neimeyer, Robert. *Techniques of Grief Therapy: Creative Practices for Counseling the Bereaved.* New York: Routledge, 2012.

Okun, Barbara, and Joseph Nowinski. *Saying Goodbye: How Families Can Find Renewal through Loss.* New York: Berkley Books, 2011.

Reina, Dennis, and Michelle Reina. *Rebuilding Trust in the Workplace: Seven Steps to Renew Confidence, Commitment, and Energy.* San Francisco: Berrett-Koehler Publishers, 2010.

Reiss, Michele A. *Lessons in Loss and Living: Hope and Guidance for Confronting Serious Illness and Grief.* New York: Hyperion, 2010.

Reivich, Karen, and Andrew Shatté. *The Resilience Factor: 7 Keys to Finding Your Inner Strength and Overcoming Life's Hurdles.* New York: Three Rivers Press, 2002.

Sandberg, Sheryl, and Adam Grant. *Option B: Facing Adversity, Building Resilience, and Finding Joy.* New York: Alfred A. Knopf, 2017.

Savary, Louis M., and Patricia H. Berne. *You Are God's Gift to the World: The Purpose of Your Life on Earth.* Bloomington, IN: Balboa Press, 2013.

Schwarz, Roger M. *The Skilled Facilitator: A Comprehensive Resource for Consultants, Facilitators, Managers, Trainers and Coaches.* Hoboken, NJ: Wiley, 2017.

Seligman, Martin E. P. *Flourish: A Visionary New Understanding of Happiness and Well-Being*. New York: Free Press, 2012.

Shafir, Rebecca Z. *The Zen of Listening: Mindful Communication in the Age of Distraction*. Wheaton, IL: Quest Books, 2000.

Study Circles Resource Center. *The Study Circle Handbook: A Manual for Study Circle, Discussion Leaders, Organizers and Participants*. Pomfret, CT: Topsfield Foundation, 1993.

Sullenberger, Chesley B. III. *Sully: The Untold Story behind the Miracle on the Hudson*. New York: William Morrow, 2009.

Van der Kolk, Bessel. *The Body Keeps the Score: Brain, Mind, and Body in the Healing of Trauma*. New York: Viking Press, 2014. Citations from the Penguin 2015 edition.

Wicks, Robert J. *Bounce: Living the Resilient Life*. New York: Oxford University Press, 2010.

Wilson, John P. *The Posttraumatic Self: Restoring Meaning and Wholeness to Personality*. New York: Routledge, 2006.

Wortmann, Craig. *What's Your Story? Using Stories to Ignite Performance and Be More Successful*. Chicago: Kaplan Publishing, 2006.

Zayfert, Claudia, and Jason C. DeViva. *When Someone You Love Suffers from Posttraumatic Stress: What to Expect and What You Can Do*. New York: Guilford Press, 2011.

Index

~

About the Author

Dr. Barbara Barski-Carrow's work focuses on relationships in the workplace. She brings to this issue more than thirty years of experience in a variety of management, administrative, and technical positions in the government and public and private sector. Her research, presentations, workshops, conferences, and publications of popular and professional articles have earned her international acclaim. In 2003, she was featured in a *Wall Street Journal* article relating to workplace issues.

Her roots are from Northeastern Pennsylvania, graduating from Wilkes University with a BA in social science/urban affairs. She relocated to Washington, D.C., and worked for the Department of Energy and Department of Health and Human Services (HHS).

At HHS she became the acting director of the Office of Equal Employment Opportunity/Office of the Secretary. In this position she created, designed, and implemented the award-winning Sexual Harassment Program, training over 1,200 employees in the headquarters and regional offices.

She holds an MA in organizational behavior/management from Georgetown University and a PhD in adult learning and human resource development from Virginia Polytechnic Institute.

She served on the faculty of the Northern Virginia Community College, Mt. Vernon College, Washington, D.C. She has been affiliated with The Women's Center, Vienna, Virginia; Department of Defense; the William Wendt Center for Loss & Healing, Washington, D.C.; and has given workshops at the Jungian Society in Washington, D.C.

She resides in Milton, Delaware, and is associated with the Cancer Consortium of Delaware; the Rehoboth Art League of Delaware; and is on the Board of Home of the Brave, Milford, Delaware; and is president of Carrow Associates.